THE KING'S FLUTE

KOSTES PALAMAS

THE KING'S FLUTE

Translated
with an Introduction
by Frederic Will

UNIVERSITY OF NEBRASKA PRESS · LINCOLN

Library of Congress Catalog card number: 66-20064

Manufactured in the United States of America

For my mother

Contents

Introduction

I

KOSTES PALAMAS provided the introduction to an introduction when he wrote " *The Twelve Words of the Gypsy* are the propylaea through which we enter into *The King's Flute*."[1] He thereby interrelated his two great epics. A capable Greek critic, reading Palamas' intention fully, elaborated the image:

> He [Palamas] is letting us know that *The King's Flute* carries the greater weight, that it is his main poetic temple, with the altars, the statues, and the paintings of his ultimate poetic ideas; with the achieved and translucent symbols which taken together indicate the unity of his "position" within the Greek and the human world. As a matter of fact, *The King's Flute* is a work, really a gesture, of "universal vision."[2]

[1] Prologue to Vol. I of his *Πεζοὶ Δρόμοι*. For *The Twelve Words of the Gypsy* in English, see my translation: *The Twelve Words of the Gypsy* (Lincoln: University of Nebraska Press, 1964). I have tried to avoid repeating here the biographical and critical remarks included in my introduction to that translation.

[2] Andreas Karantones, *Γύρω στὸν Παλαμᾶ, Πρώτη Σειρά* (Athens, 1959), p. 177.

First impressions, admittedly, may seem to contradict this statement. *The King's Flute* is bound, as *The Twelve Words* was not, to historical detail. True, *The Twelve Words* was set in the mid-fourteenth century; but the temporal foci are fuzzy. Even the locale, whether around The City, Constantinople, or moving toward The City, through one of the provinces, was smudged and kinetic, while the Gypsy himself, narrator and central figure, existed essentially outside history, as an exemplar of eternal powers and awarenesses in man.

The King's Flute, by contrast, seems much more bound to historical detail. It does, in fact, concern real people and real events to a degree unknown in *The Twelve Words*. The protagonist is the eleventh-century Byzantine emperor Basil II, the Bulgar-killer. The theme or frame for feeling is Basil's journey through Greece to Athens, to worship the Virgin Mary in her cathedral, the Christianized Parthenon. The epic is a historical narrative.

From the beginning, though, this history has been organically widened out into myth and visionary panorama. The tale has been recounted by a magic flute, found in the mouth of the corpse of Basil. That flute chants the epic, which is thus heightened to a visionary document of Basil's time and experience. The experience is both generally Greek and generally human. That which is generally Greek, here, is finally only explainable by this—or a comparable—poem. It cannot be isolated. Some of its features, though, let themselves be baldly stated.

Mary, a transformation but continuation of Athena, is the center of the poem. Her grace radiates in all directions from her. It draws to her, with warmth felt already at the beginning, a hero—and heroic entourage—which are in their way brutal. Basil has slaughtered: but like the *preux chevaliers* of Western epic, like Roland or Rinaldo, he has slaughtered in the shadow of the labarum, for the glory of God. He is one of Mary's warriors.

Greek this is, in one sense of that complex word; chiefly Byzantine Greek, to be exact. Where it is Byzantine Greek, however, it manages in a surprising way also to become generally human. Here we touch the mystery of that phase of human spirit which the Rome of the East fostered in the High Middle Ages and to which Palamas was so attuned. Byzantine Greek comes here to connote that high point of a civilization at which pomp, brutality, and majesty intersect most firmly with the need for divine compassion. Palamas was a master at plotting this intersection.

II

In a long poem built so unashamedly about atmosphere, and so negligent of articulated plot, it is difficult even to find the main lines of the theme; and it is one job of an introduction to make those lines a little more conspicuous. They are schematically arranged in the chapter plot-summaries which Palamas himself provided, but I have omitted these from my translation; it seemed more useful to try to assemble the whole picture here, compactly and in one place.

The prologue is addressed to the heroism hidden at all times in men's creative hearts, yet temporarily—and the reference seems to be chiefly to Palamas' own day—silenced or at best muffled. The nineties of the last century, during which much of the epic was being written, were hard years for Greece. Unsuccessful struggles against Balkan neighbors and severe military losses to Turkey were heavy weights on a new—and always proud—nation which was determined to make its modern reincarnation great. National creativity was crucial, and at stake to a degree that frightened such anxious and prophetic tempers as Palamas. The following epic, he implies, will be a vast exhortation.

From that point he moves us into the density of

history, into an obscure but portentous moment in Basil's history: when as a youth, being taken with other prisoners of the Bulgars, he confronts the Bulgarian Tzar, who hopes to train him as manservant, saddler, staff holder. The unimpressed boy retorts:

> My Lord, your staff's too heavy for my hands
> and as for armor, what I happen on
> I'll wear on my own frame.
> My mother never taught
> me metal-polishing,
> so in your armory I'd simply
> waste my time.

The first two Words or cantos of the epic move leapingly to The City, Constantinople; and though their emphases are different, both give us the world of that Eastern capital as a (or as a chief) viewing-point onto the rest of the epic. The First Word puts us in the mid-fourteenth century—during Michael Paleologos' siege of Constantinople, which was at that time still held by Frankish Crusaders. Some of Michael's soldiers happen upon ruins, and there discover a skeleton, identified by epigraph as that of the Emperor Basil II. In the skeleton's mouth is a flute. Amazed, they proceed to remove the instrument, whereupon it begins to sound and chants into the tale of Basil's life:

An infinite enchantment poured, as though
the world and all it was had turned to silence
on all sides, and all had changed,
become a single mouth, its voice, the song they wove.

The Second Word sets and consecrates the scene on which the eleventh-century events of the epic occur. We stand inside The City; or rather among that evil, gorgeous, beseeching, and Mary-adoring royalty which staffed the Byzantine court in the eleventh century. (The actual physical scene is on those fated Prinkipo islands, in the bay to the southeast of The City, to which many princes were ultimately exiled.) The doomed but mighty specter-characters—like Augusta Theophano—ready us for the tremendous, flawed Basil of Word Three. Palamas' sense of relevant atmosphere is at its most luxurious in this particular " readying."

In Word Three we are under way, following Basil on a route of conquests through the eastern Mediterranean and northern Greece; through those mouthy heapings of river and city names which Palamas loved; through

the Kaukasos, the Nile, the Apennines,
the Tauros and the Antitauros.
And from the Sava to the Winter Mountains,
all his own monocracy
up to the Balkans.

Under way also means " in mind of Athens, the Parthenon, and Mary," who are brought increasingly, toward that Word's end, into the center of awareness. *We* are made aware of them, and by the *narrator*; yet it is felt that *Basil's* consciousness is gradually filling with these presences, as he nears.

The Fourth Word, if possible more sumptuously verbal than the Third, names and numbers the armies assembled under Basil. Word Five is Greece, and for Greece, that " genetic land." The extent of land, before the descending Basil, is laid out in language like this, with which the presentation of Thessaly begins:

> Your earth is polycarp, river-nursed,
> your fields are dew and rich, your passes broad,
> your grassy richness flowers, whiffs like honey
> for your herds to graze in,
> to increase and harvest.
> Like your polycarp earth
> Imagination in you
> bore fruit
> sweetfused with Hellenic thought . . .

and on and on, into the conjoined arteries of an immensely sustained lyric sentence. The Word culminates with Mount Parnassos, passionately addressing Basil and his troops,

. . . you who pass so grandly from here
before whose treading the earth is shaken, trembles;
immeasurable, sudden people, led
by a pitiless Hero, a king, cavalier . . . .

Palamas is one of the few twentieth-century masters of pathetic fallacy.

To this vision of reception, Word Six adds chiefly the impression of receiving and joyful crowds, elbowing their way toward points in the Greek land from which they can see and worship Basil, the Emperor, Savior.

Athena and the Parthenon speak and are spoken to—by the poet—in Word Seven. A vast peroration to the queen of Doric temples,

. . . simple,
great to the triple degree,
its thinnest line drawn true . . .

opens. Then Athena speaks, ruminating on the changed world in which she finds herself, finally questioning the identity of the army and leader whom she visions, and above all feels, coming down the plain toward her.

" I behold; the tread of an army; I behold the brilliance
of weapons. Crosses and eagles, shields and spears,
and labara,
and from all the clouding up
no bursting epiphany,
Homeric god . . ."

but rather, as she goes on into realizing, a *new* Ares, who " longed for the goddess."

By the beginning of Word Seven we have felt the oncoming of a head-on meeting: Basil and Athena. At such moments, as here in Word Eight, Palamas shifts perspective. Now he will give a sense of the depth and continuity behind the Byzantine spirituality of Basil and of his age. Two dramas are offered. In the first, which follows an old legend, the neo-Platonic philosopher Proklos (*ca.* 500 A.D.) is visited, in dream, by Athena. She reports on her forthcoming expulsion; on Mary, the new goddess; and on the changing of times. Later—in the second drama—we are in a Near Eastern monastery, sometime in the higher Middle Ages, and are introduced into moments of a saintly monk's life; into the life of a man

> . . . apart though among
> the other *fratres*, a cypress feeling
> apart among the bentbranch willows,
> higher, lither, darker, with a certain
> mystic motion, incomparable grace; that one.

His mysterious end, oddly enough, has prepared us to understand Basil more fully.

In Word Nine Basil has reached the Doric temple, has come within both the end of his pilgrimage and the temple of himself; there

he flies with prayer's wings;
and that prayer is strange, bears on its wings
a warjoy flame, a mystic dew.

In the following interiorization, he lays his past before Mary. His struggles for power, and the growth of his understanding, are outspread in an immense offering, the kind of offering in syntax which Palamas' whole *oeuvre* itself sometimes appears to be.

Word Ten continues the autobiography; the inner history of Basil's struggle against Bardas the Hard, mentor, then rival of the young ruler. Crowning Basil's own successes, finally, come the objects of booty, the things brought in words to the Queen of Creation:

the booty of Achrid, Prilepi, and Prespa;
the vases outpouring with golden
denarii;
rugs of Damaskos, the purple weft . . . .

Word Eleven is prophecy, as is some thrust in all Palamas' major work. Here we have Basil as explicitly grand-style visionary—like the Gypsy as prophet in *The Twelve Words of the Gypsy*—and with him we see the emergences of new, more modern powers: of Mammon, of America, of socialism, and finally, in one of its inevitable rebirths, of that Hellenism which he represents, which is at once Christian and pagan, warlike and compassionate, wherever and in whatever place,

> whether Polis in some huge land, where world
> is of lands and of oceans, of people and places,
> or in hut of a slave, in a cell-low land,
> in the midst of tables of gold, in the wolf's isolation,
> on Byzantine thrones or in Attic ruins,
> in the purple of kings, in a stolen cloak,
> wherever are opposition and cross and wakefulness,
> sword and the road . . . .

Word Twelve completes it. The flute has finished its song. The Emperor Michael Paleologos comes, bearing gifts for Basil's second funeral, a funeral "more splendid than the first." He reaches out toward Basil's skeleton:

> In vain. The instant your hands make contact
> the remains fall heaped on the ground,
> fall ground themselves. And onto them
> dumbed, the flute of the Muses, a reed
> for throwing away.

The Twelve Words of the Gypsy, as I see it, has a good many soft spots, and in writing the introduction to my translation of that epic, I tried to touch those spots. They were points at which rhetoric and abstraction got the better of Palamas, and the language was drained of substance.

I read *The King's Flute* differently. Much less is specifically memorable in it than in *The Twelve*

Words, but it operates on a more consistent level of poetic coercion. Its digressions—into Basil's past, into the life of the holy monk, into presenting such figures as Augusta Theophano—all prompt the reader to a firmer affective grasp of the "argument." Its projection of thrust—toward Athens, the Parthenon, and Mary—is felt everywhere, furnishing an implicit directional energy it never relinquishes. The City, Constantinople, plays the same axial role in *The Twelve Words*, but there all geography is metaphored far more than in *The King's Flute*. In the earlier work, meaninglessly unlocalized events are always threatening the movement of the whole.

The single episodes of *The King's Flute* cannot be dismissed as unmemorable, even when allowance is made for Palamas' not wanting to create, here, what we might call memorable scenes. Much *does* stay in precision: the meeting of young Basil with the Bulgarian Tzar, the specters moving on Prinkipo Island, the pouring of troops down over the Greek landscape, the speech by Mount Parnassos, the first glimpses of the Parthenon, Basil's description of his relation to Bardas the Hard, and much else. I wonder, though, whether even in these, the hardest and clearest episodes, the ear, and behind it the mind's intuition, are not working far harder than the eye; far harder than is customary, that is, even in an art like poetry, where the eye normally works only as an interior sense.

The special unity and completeness of *The King's Flute* result from its consistent address to the ear-as-mind. A liturgical tone results, and is maintained with unremitting finesse. The work streams ahead, an enormous river of prayer and adoration, continually deflected—though never meandering—into tributaries which invariably, through marsh, stream, or delta, find their way back to the sea of compassion, to the Lady. What we know and hear, under the things seen and done, is the prayer to Her.

III

Translating this epic, as the foregoing suggests, has been " more than usually difficult." A good distinction has been made between translation and transposition. The former is required, on this theory, when the two language-cultures involved in the transaction are far apart. The culture from which the translation is being made, in that case, requires pretty thorough reinterpretation and refashioning. Transposition, on the other hand, could take place between language-cultures which were fairly akin, as, say, modern French and modern English. Palamas' Greek lies at some hard-to-focus middle distance from our English.

His Greek archaizes, in several ways. He is consciously rhetorical, often unashamedly—though complexly—grand; and he is addicted to an immensely widespread vocabulary, which draws its richness from ancient and Byzantine as much as from modern strata of the language. (Even to try to match this last dexterity in an English poem, we would need to sprinkle our text with actual, unchanged words from Old and Middle English.) And of course his created mood is as far as possible purely Byzantine. *It* is ancient.

At the same time, Palamas manages to be modern in several of the senses we give that word when it is applied to poetry. He writes shaggy lines, sometimes, of variable lengths and variable stress patterns, although his stock line is the fifteen-syllable political verse-line, traditionally Greek. He distorts his syntax, sometimes consciously refuses to complete sentences, maintains acute oral tenseness. Above all, he links sentences, paragraphs, and cantos by chains so delicate, unpredictable, and long that one at times feels almost too much in the poet's hands.

That modernity I have tried to keep, though

always against its darker, sumptuous historical backdrop. I have had more trouble, however, meeting the mode in which Palamas projects both his ancient and his modern voices. The problem of the rhetorical has constantly badgered me. It is, I suppose, the traditionally Greek element in Palamas to which it is hardest for us to reconcile ourselves. No simple principles of harmonizing, of literary moderation, have worked here. I have had to rely, as far as I could, on the tact of the moment. Three examples will help to show how much too little this was.

Often in Palamas the rhetorical springs from an old passion for names. Homer catalogues ships and warriors; Aischylos, in the *Agamemnon*, names the geographical points relaying to Argos the beacon-news of victory at Troy; Theokritos names the flowers of the shepherds' fields. Behind Palamas, and moving squarely through Byzantine homily and epics like *Digenes Akritas*, worked a tradition of name-sounds into which Palamas eagerly stepped.

Basil's address to the Virgin Mary, at the end of Word Ten, provides a classic outlet for this national name-pressure. Basil offers back, to Mary, the countless names of her which she has provided for her worshipers throughout the Empire. They are the names I have translated into:

All Queen, Who Pities.
Lover in Sweetness, Ubiquitous, Healer, Freer
There, Seer, Fulfiller, Leader,
Who Answers,
Noonsun,
Swift in Response,
Romaic, Athenian, Seen,
Tower goldwoven, throne suntarred

but they are not easily translatable. For one thing, the Greek tradition, being on this matter a tradition, can support a longer list, can rely on a higher level of aural tolerance for names. In translating the present list, I have omitted two of the Greek epithets. Much more has been shorn from the tropically rich meanings of the Greek words. Their roots are in many cases sunk into a past which to us is at most a book-learned abstraction. My " Ubiquitous " translates *akathiste*, a word meaning literally " unseated," " without defined location," and applied, originally, to the unseated singers of the hymn. By Palamas, however, metaphysical implication is acquired from a word meaning literally " unseated," but taught through centuries of usage into a finer meaning, and into a transplanted reference. Here, the Virgin is " placeless," " ubiquitous." The Greek word behind my

" Swift in Response " is equally inaccessible. " Gorgoepekoos " does mean " swift in hearing and responding," but it means it " embodiedly." (Much more than *I* realize, many of these other epithets may contain their meanings " embodiedly.") " Gorgoepekoos " means itself in terms of the experience of a particular church, a Byzantine jewel of Athens, still called the Church of the Virgin who is " Gorgoepekoos." Thus it takes on its meaning in terms of habitual, deeply seeped experiences of which some, at least, would be commemorated in each Athenian's reading of this epithet in Palamas. " Swift in Response " goes, as we say, only so far. All the larger sumptuousness of sound, the vowelled color, is also lacking to my collection of epithets, but from that more obvious weakness I turn to a second instance.

Palamas' rhetoric includes what to our ears may often seem a shameless inclination to pathetic fallacy. Almost this entire epic is the speech of a flute. Throughout it, voices of weapons, rivers, and mountains are heard. What can we do, in today's English, with a mountain's peroration to passing troops? Part of what I have done with it, the speech by Mount Parnassos in Word Five, is the following:

And you who pass so grandly from here
before whose treading the earth is shaken, trembles;
immeasurable, sudden people, led
by a pitiless Hero, a king, cavalier
apart, worth you all—
the sweat of a thousand journeys drops from your
  bodies,
in your eyes burn fires of a thousand wars;
it is as though you went—not as before
to ruins and bleeding, suddenly, fatally—
but somewhere else, joyful, and festal,
to religious worship, the festal;
advance, and hear me, people, and break your course
come here and bend, bend genuflect,
bend worthy before your god, whatever god,
from my twin peaks.

The tact of the moment, as I have said, is my guide here. Principles fall before the effort to match such high-style language as this Greek. Here as usual the Greek lines are long (fifteen-stress), complete, and orotund; my longest and fullest lines—the second and sixth in this passage—are shorter, lack the vowelled openness of the Greek, and threaten to break down from inner anemia. Whereas my shortest lines, like the fifth, are often only admissions of defeat. What was I to do, in that case, with the Greek line:

<table>
<tr><td>who</td><td>separates off</td><td>from</td><td>all of you</td><td>and</td><td>is worth</td></tr>
<tr><td>pou</td><td>xechoridzee</td><td>ap</td><td>olous</td><td>sas ki</td><td>axidsei</td></tr>
<tr><td></td><td></td><td>that</td><td></td><td>one</td><td>all of you</td></tr>
<tr><td></td><td></td><td>o</td><td></td><td>enas</td><td>olous.</td></tr>
</table>

I can hear it said that I should have written " who stands apart from you all, and is worth you all." Not a bad alternative, but one that I avoid to escape that piling of monosyllables which tire in extended English poetry, and for the sake of variation in line length—one of the little strategies I find operative in the shaping of each section of the poem. At another point, this Greek line offers no room for compensation. In its syntactical excitement, peculiar to an inflected, and thus syntactically flexible, language, *o enas* is the subject of *axidsei*, which it follows—already a difficult relation for English—yet *o enas* has been prepared by the preceding *pou*, to which it is in apposition, though their kinship is tensely withheld by the intervening verb. Finally, *o enas* and *olous* are syntactically jammed together, though they are opposed both in meaning, here, and in case—the accusative of *olous* being truly " accused "—in such a way that the punch of the line is greatly reinforced by its syntax. Before all this, I repeat, no specific compensation seems possible, only some larger redesigning.

My third example, of the point where Palamas' rhetoric grows unreachable, is simpler but harder. At the beginning of Word Eight the Parthenon, as the home of Mary, the new Athena, is panegyrized. Suddenly we are at the foot of the Acropolis, in the house of Proklos, the Neo-Platonic philosopher; it is 500 A.D., and the realm of legend. A knock at the door; there stands Athena, just driven out by Mary, seeking a night's lodging, a brief sleep during which a change of cultures can descend onto the world. The tone of the meeting evades my best effort, this:

> Proklos, at home. All night awake.
> Wakelessness choked him, the fall
> came whipping, thinking consumed him.
> The middle of night. A knock.
> All ears!—Who knocks?—
> He listens. The trembling of voice.
> " Make ready the house. Receive her.
> The Lady is coming.
> Will stay with you now."
>
> " I have no way to go, no shelter from night.
> Let me sleep here, and leave, at dawn,
> swiftly in flight with swallows and cranes.
> Driven from my creation. Stranger
> and outcast on my own throne
> in my own possessions.
> Madness the way *she* came,
> inclined, and humble,
> that evil magicianness, ach! "

I take the passage to be rhetorical, through being so public, speaking out so into the common body of Greek sensibilities. In this case the sensibilities are particular to a certain Greek historical experience: here, in the Greek, the awesome and the arch are bafflingly fused. What remains in English, I think, stresses the archness—in the "*she*" and the "ach!"—but fails to translate awe. It is hard for us to mix these ingredients.

What I have tried to do, as compensation throughout this translation, is suggested by what I have tried in this Proklos passage. The "ach!" and the "she" run the risk of suggesting a jealous housewife, arms akimbo or wrists flapping. To encourage at least a partially grave historical awareness I have forced the word "fall" (l. 2), the expression "make ready the house" (l. 7), and the word "creation" (l. 13). The first two expressions, in the Greek, mean more nearly "driving-out" and "receive her!," but by my theologically auraed translation I hope to import an otherwise lost gravity into the passage. *Plase*, the Greek word behind my "creation," here probably refers only to the Parthenon. I have allowed that single sense to remain, but crowded, as I think English usage guarantees, with awareness of the vastness of Athena's loss.

The cunning of the translator, I think, is shockingly dependent on such local compensations. Bag of tricks in hand, the translator seasons his new work with magics unknown to the original. He tries to make up for the original's losses. The Greekless reader of my translation will, of course, not know where or how I have tried to accomplish this. It is perhaps indiscreet to tell him, but it may finally heip if I elaborate on a couple of my methods for trying to make up loss.

Importation of new meanings has rarely been attempted here, even to the degree shown above, in the Proklos passage. I have made no effort to reinterpret Palamas' poem, and very little special effort even to make it sound like a poem in English. At most daring, words like my " fall " and " creation," above, meet Greek halfway, and bring out a sense latent in them, at the same time as making them English. I think it will be clear that I take pleasure, here, in a controlled stiffness and strangeness of meaning.

Yet Palamas' meanings, as the remarks on his rhetoric probably showed, are not isolatable from the way he means them; and the way he means them, his rhetorical way, has virtues in Greek which are nonexistent in English. His way would be easier in French, and in fact wants describing in the terms of classical French criticism: it is the way of *grandeur*, *souffle*, *nobilité*.

We lack in English even a tradition of that kind, though Whitman, Eliot, and Crane have all proven the modern powers of extended English verse. Above all we—and by " we " I mean our ears—are suspicious readers of grand verse. I have not only shorn much of the rhetorical sound of Palamas, in translating him, but I have tried to give it back to my readers in a tone they could accept—though not without some effort, I hope.

A look at typography suggests the basic shift of emphasis. Palamas seldom deviates here—as he did so often and so brilliantly in *The Twelve Words*—from the fifteen-stress political line. Nor, almost incredibly in an epic of over four thousand lines, does he ever lose his sense of the dignity and autonomy of the line (in this resembling Homer, and drawing, perhaps, on the unique adequacy of the clause in Greek). The sense of the line, of course, I have tried to preserve. But the marble-block lines of Palamas have been far too heavy and completed for me. The lines of my translation are jagged as old teeth.

This way, I hope, led in English to greater excitement. Let me illustrate briefly. Word Five culminates with the speech, quoted above, addressed by Mount Parnassos to Basil's troops. In these brief lines, Parnassos prepares to sing:

> And Parnassos has heard the passing, and watches
> the people,
> and opens itself a song—for it is entirely song,
> a song to remain unsilenced,
> a song from root to peak, like the Flute myself.

And mouths and lyres sang out that song
the mouths of
all that bloom and fly and stir and stay
on the mountain's slopes and passes
and caves and peaks . . . .

The Greek passage is foursquare, consisting of only six lines, all of nearly the same length. It is a chunk of language. I have tried to aerate it and break it up, providing more variety and excitement. I think our ears require that. This is part of what I understand as the translator's effort at compensation.

This passage in English happens to contain one line, the second, which illustrates a second kind of compensation. The bulk of my passage is roughly iambic, or iambic-stretched-toward-anapaestic (such parlance being, of course, only a gross approximation to the actual pattern of stresses). The Greek here is much more sinuous and irregular than even my English: it is more closely built on conversation, hence in a way on prose, than the English, but it is built on the strangely flexible, pitched pattern of Greek conversation. The Greek is inaccessible, the best English equivalent is generally iamb-based; but to avoid the dullness of repeated iambs, compensatory prosodic techniques are urgently necessary. I have used them freely.

The most common illustrate themselves in the second line here, where jamming of stressed syllables is suggested in the

for it is entirely song,

a passage readable either iambically or, as marked here, jammed, and actually serving simply to thicken the kind of line which in extended English verse of this sort can become colorless and textureless. Some such thickening is also intended in the " all that bloom," five lines farther down. The following six lines, addressed by Basil to the Virgin, offer an unusually dense collection of stresses:

> And from all the names you took from all
> those places, your wonders, your particular graces,
> names raying like your brow's glory,
> balsam like your own countenance
> deep like the springs of pity and mercy
> which are your two eyes . . . .

My stress marks, in these cases, are intended merely as nudgings. They seemed useful as warnings against the old iambic mood into which most of us can imperceptibly fall, losing all sense of the character of our reading. They keep us on guard against a mere conversational reading.

IV

When I was writing about the mediaeval cultural history of the Parthenon, a few years ago, I asked Mr. Philip Sherrard for bibliographical advice, and by a (for me) happy chance he sent me toward *The King's Flute*. That was the beginning; on that warm Athens night I first heard of a poem about Basil and Mary. Thanks.

It would be futile to try listing those who have helped with the job since then. Too many people helped too indirectly for present inclusion. I will stick to essentials.

Eugène Clément, French translator of *The King's Flute*, as well as of *The Twelve Words of the Gypsy*, has been over the ground of Palamas' text and translated it with accuracy and a strangely living prose. There is no word of his translation that I haven't considered, for confirmation or consolation.

His text of *The King's Flute* was brought to my hands and hungry eyes by Mr. George Katsimbalis, once a Colossus of Maroussi, but to me more nearly a guardian angel. During the past months, Mr. Katsimbalis, whom I have met only once or twice, has unsolicitedly kept my mailbox full: with the newest edition of Palamas' *opera omnia*, with critical works on the poet, and with much more. It would be hard to overstress the importance to me, locked in an Iowa winter, of these documents from the Mediterranean.

For help received in and during this landlocked winter, much gratitude to other Greeks both in Greece and far from home. Among those in Greece, I remain in constant and affectionate debt to Popi Bodouroglou and Nelly Andrikopoulou. The Iowa City Greek community, like most of the Hellenic diaspora in this country, keeps its culture and mind sharpened: I am especially grateful, for help rendered, to Mrs. Alexios Toszkas, Mrs. Mary Gregory, Miss Kathi Papastathopoulos, Professor Stavros Deligiorgis, Professor John Fertis, and Mr. Stamatios Krimidzis. All have put their hermeneutic eyes to the Palamas text and helped me with its riddles. Mr. George Arnakis and Mr. Edmund Keeley have read and criticized this introduction, to my great advantage—and perhaps to their despair, considering how much good advice I have willfully overlooked. To their good insights my wife has, as always, added hers. And her love. Finally, the Translation Workshop, of which I have been director, at the University of Iowa. This extraordinary program in applied translation has helped me to subject my principles and practice to a scrutiny as intelligent as any teacher is likely to receive from his students—from students, in this case, who were the true *magistri*.

FREDERIC WILL

Kostes Palamas: A Brief Chronology

1859	Born in Patras on January 13. His father, John Palamas, was a judge.
1866–1874	Upon the death of his parents when he was seven, he was sent to Missolonghi to be reared by his uncle Demetrios. Received a gymnasium education in Missolonghi.
1875	Went to Athens to study law at the University of Athens, but quit the University without completing a degree.
1880–1885	Worked in Athens as a newspaperman and literary critic. Became allied with the cause of the Demotikistes, a group which favored the use of the popular idiom in literature rather than the classical Greek of the purists.
1886	First volume of poems, *Songs of My Fatherland* published.
	Married Maria Valvi from Missolonghi. They had three children: Nausika, Leandros, and Alki.
1892	Publication of *Eyes of My Soul.*
1895	*A Man's Death*, one of his best-known short stories, published in the *Hestia*, an Athens daily.

1897	Appointed secretary general of the University of Athens, a post which he held until his retirement in 1926.
1898	Wrote *The Tomb*, his most famous lyric poem, after the death of his nine-year-old son Alki.
1906	Publication of his translation of Emile Verhaeren's lyric drama *Helen of Sparta.*
1907	*The Twelve Words of the Gypsy.*
1910	*The King's Flute.*
1930	*Reaccented Music*, a volume of poetry, published.
1943	Died in Athens on February 9.

THE KING'S FLUTE

PROLOGUE

Darkened all creative lights in the land.
In church, on forge, in homes, in factories,
everywhere,
in the castle and in the heart,
half burnt fragments, ashes.
The baker leaves, the worker-in-bronze, the wife,
the young men go, the priests and the
   rhythm-workers,
and the Prophets of the Word.
Hands are paralyzed, and the hammers gone
and none to hammer the chariots and plows.
And if some fermenter's palm encloses
some yeasting grain
no soul will find that seed to make it bread.
The hearth is full of
cold ash
and more than the hearth which is the house's
   heart
the heart of man has come to evil. Pity. Pity.
The church black ruin, the fort
without crenelations,
turned to grass for cattle.
Love is far
away, and man is lost, and lost to act.
And at his side degraded wife

possessing her slavery and her slave—untruth.
Darkened all creative lights in the land.
Song of the heroes! Forward, song of the heroes!
Above the incinerated world, illumine, lighten,
flame!
You'll see no hand outspread above you,
to nourish you, to take your warmth, to take
your strength,
to place you again at church, at forge, at home,
to nurse you in some heart, or camp, or factory.
And flame you will hide yourself in helplessness,
isolation;
but hide yourself in ash, and do not go out.

Because a time will come, a dawn will burst,
a wind of unknown power come blowing: listen!
From what mouth or chaos it will pour I cannot
say.
It may come from the east, it may come from
the west,
or from the north, or from the south;
may be cast from hell, from interstellar space.
I cannot say: I know that it will come, and with
its passing—
great and holy, strange, and indescribable—
summits will bow their pines, the fires be
relighted.

At church, on forge, in homes, in factories,
at camp, in hearts; everywhere—among the
ruins—
an April!
And behold the baker now, and the worker-in-
bronze,
and the woman—see her now!—
and the young men, and the priests, and the
rhythm-workers
and the Prophets of the Word
like shaped and thaumaturgic forms of gods
they ring with music, with the simple kiss of
Sun the lord,
like green shade-heavy trees,
never—in winter or summer—left by sugar
perfect fruits.
And when on every side the creative flames
relight
resume your own life, flame;
Resume it flame and cast
yourself, go forward into the stretches of city,
the crevasses of the soul,
and form and live them all,
and fill the beating hearts of flourishing youths,
and shape and live through certain fathering
longings,
and shape and live through certain thoughts as
mothers,

make deeds and dreams be brothers! Forward,
song!

Darkened all the lights, a song of heroes!

THE WIDOW'S SON

An edict from the Kroutagos, Bulgaria's Tzar:

Freedom he grants to his slaves and home to
those
in foreign parts; a curse on Kroumos the enslaver!
Twenty years they have blanched
in foreign darkness; men
grown old, the young men turned to men,
children
into leventes, to mothers the baby girls. All
passes.
Triply cursed their agings, cursed that youth
that flows and comes to fruit in foreign lands,
enslaved.
But times have changed, the earth has eaten
Kroumos.
The wise Theophilos now rules the City,
the sword of Kroumos hangs, consumed to rust.
An edict from the Kroutagos, Bulgaria's Tzar.
Slowly they go like flocks; slowly the slaves and
exiles
going. Enthroned above them, the watching Tzar.
Women with children, ancient men with staffs,
and from the heaviness of the carrying, young men,

the architecture of your bodies bends and groans.
And the virgin goes in shame inside her rags.
Hunger advances, misfortune, nakedness, dread.
And the dewcool flowers of beauty burned
by slavery's tragic sun. And the noblest
men rubbed down by servitude
debased by suffering.
If ever the enslaver came on roses, he kept
them for his,
and the slave had thorns to fill his dreams.
And sun, how you shone on him without
warming,
shadow, how you chilled him without cooling.
And all go forward, all enslaved go straight
ahead,
and sometimes they half-smile, and sometimes
groan,
and mingle sorrows of slavery with hope of a
fatherland;
deep in their groanings, in their bitter laughing.

Keep your patience longer, consume more road,
under another heaven another soil, you'll tread
and cut the clovers then, and there the heat
of the sun will warm like some mothering summit.
You will drink the dew. Each beauty,
fatherland, will be in your hands.

Idolatrous and heartless Kroutagos, the Tzar.
Just yesterday he offered the crown—the
martyr's crown—to Manuel the Saint.
But now the joy of God has dawned
as though it touched him, he greets the secret joy
of dispensing freedom;
and oblation from the graceless world of slaves.
Out there they pass, and bend, and stumble.
Only a single one goes by who never bends,
who never stumbles.
He is no giant in his body, in years no man.
Yesterday he played with children's toys.
But now! Straight and lofty, fine and noble,
a journeyer without a care, a sharp leventes,
his costume noble and his glance tomorrow;
embroidered golden eagles on his coat.
You meet him and you know he does not know
the bending of the slave—which the others know—
you meet him and you know: a bloom
the sun has never scorched.
In the scorching of sun the others labored
for this one, and went poor for him
always to keep him clothed in brilliance,
as though they awaited from him
a pushing back of the stone
a resurrection.

Although near slaves, he soars.
No one would think he goes,
freed slave, from slavery home.
But rather returns from war
to an awaiting throne.
This man alone refuses to kneel
or bend, and astounds the emperor, who asks:
" Who is that man who never bows? "
" The widow's son, a growth without example! "
" Then bring him here! "
As though blackwater spews a delirious river,
and the fields are flooded, covered, turned to
ocean,
and the river steals trees and covers the land,
and whoever has hut in that land's middle
awakes at night, hears unknown violence of land,
and has nowhere to go, no forward or backward,
because ahead are waves, and flood behind,
and he shudders, trembles, sweats and waits—
so at the gates of deliverance this race of slaves
stands shuddering; trembles, sweats, and waits
through this frightful impeding of the widow's son.
And the people cannot go forward because he
leaves them,
and the people cannot go backward, for slavery
is there.
A suffocated voice is heard:
" My holy God! My wretched brothers,

the princely son, that
only son will not return,
my god, he'll rot his strength in Bulgar work."
His mother crumbles, a lightning battered heap,
broken groanings shatter.
Moanings, shriekings spread on the air,
they whip the empty air,
and hands outspread and tear
out fistsful of hair by the roots,
thousands of glances rivet
to the throne of the Kroutagos
and approach the Tzar
and beg him in hopelessness:
" We in our freedom cannot have
our strength a distant slave;
better that chains should eat
our lives forever! "
And the livened thought caught on
spread from human to human.
So the northwind piles the waves on each other:
" Let us not be free
without him; better
that irons eat our lives forever! "
Who is the son of the widow, who, the
  musknursed prince,
desire of an entire people, idol;
and if Kroutagos holds him, what evil will
  follow?

(Cut out your path
my epic's sword of speech
and take the road of an earlier day.
Be on!)

It was a harvest day, in the hour of noon,
the scattered field in the barely sweetest
  movement,
like cradled sleeping of a blond, blond child.
The workers stopped their harvest,
a wordless instant:
there is no sound, no guzlar heard;
it is the painting of day, the silence of night.
The doves at peace take nests and sleep,
somehow falls of snow which no ray melts.
Here and there deep in the fields
the poppies stretch scarlet corollas
to the soil
as though beseeching from the land
moisture they cannot find
and the herds hide, safe from highnoon heat,
with giant coalblack eyes that shine;
herds in some perspectives like works of stone,
turned black and yellow with the going of time.
The plane trees spread their helpless shadow

as though the leaves were nailed to their branches.
The sun is a fiery serpent's eye
bewitching that infinite plumaged bird
the earth.
And everything good and strong,
supple and great,
stagnates in silence, bound in a magic.
But the widow can take no moment's rest;
in her own home queen, in slavery a harvester.
She trembles, rises, runs to see her child.
Her husband
atrophied by scorn,
she has stayed by the boy, that growth without
  a like.
And while summer pauses she spreads
a greenwhite bed
for him to sleep.
On green miraculous in that high heat
with flowers that have shed their souls
in the laurel's shadow, at the laurel's root.
But the tree is small, and look! The sun
is free, and its rays beat down
crosswise over the boy.
She sees this from far;
outcrying she goes to hold him,
sees an enormous cloud—she thinks—
which flows to earth
and seizes and yokes itself above the youth

and struggles to cloak him, to snatch him darkly,
to sleep him in deepness thickly, in shadow.
The widow staggers and groans; then shrieks.
It is no giant cloud, or blackness of fog.
Behold! A hunting eagle, a sharp-beaked eagle
widespread wings and branching claws,
a wildbeast plumage yellow, white and black.
At the woman's cry they run they race;
harvesters and their women, a race,
then workers from every side
and open a war of stones to drive the beastbird,
and the beastbird flees then turns then comes
again
and seven times they chase him and seven he
comes
back to spread his wings on the sleep of the boy.
Behold! An ancient harvester,
half-knowing in magic
and prophecies comes forward and sees and
speaks:
" Great the goodness of God, all praise to his
name;
the crosswinged eagle is sent by heavenly will.
The stork tells our spring's arrival,
and autumn—you tell us the cyclamen comes,
and fareyed eagle tells our solemn fate.
Where an owl is heard it warns of accident
where a swallow stops good luck is near,

whoever a crosswinged eagle shadows
will be king."
The speech did not expire, but another took it,
a scholar now, a man of spirit who knew the past.
He said: " Till now not five hundred years
have passed
since Vandals on Vandals flooded the world,
assaulted Rome, brought the city terror.
Gezerichos, their king and Attila's bloodbrother,
foams and batters, scatters and conquers, burns
and beats and slaughters,
encloses the imperial army, in iron traps,
inbinds it in powerful traps.
In flocks from every distance they advanced
before him,
slaves: on high Gezerichos looked down.
Gezerichos commanded: Fire to all! The knife!
And the slaves in rows await guillotine,
and one young slave does not await—he sleeps—
and the giant wings of an eagle cover him.
The astounded Vandal issues orders:
'Do not disturb the sweetness of that sleeper
Fate has named for thrones, a king.'
He gives him welcome, spares the knife and fire.
The words come true; the slave is throned as
king."
The mother came, bent above her child:
" Dear, a royal crown is for your head,

Alexander's fatherland is yours,
that greatest king who rode
Bucephalos at first and then the world.
Your father was the branch of a golden tree
and I am the tarnished stone of a holy crown.
And in your veins flows blood of Holyconstantine.
The tree of the Arsaces will spread
shoot after royal shoot
to east and west."
And still the eagle's wings were whipping the air.
Such moisture livened withered hearts
although the highnoon harvest sun was burning.
Such moisture, prophetic vision's grace
the wind's outspreading
in the joyless world of slaves.
The longwinged bird took wing and went;
but the magic of his shadow stayed and stays.
From that time on and that day on
they idolized the boy and made obeisance.
(Abandon, my epic's lyre,
the path you've taken,
and hold to your earlier route.)
And Bulgaria's Tzar, the Kroutagos, addresses
him:
"And who are you, my proud, my lord-taught
boy?"
" The widow's son am I, her one inheritor."
" Then tell me; what's your country, what's
your city?"

" Of Makedonia I am, my city Nike."
" Will you go to my palace, lad, as page,
to hold my staff, and help me put my weapons
on, to help me dress, to saddle my horse?
To earn fine money in gold? "
" May your time be long, my Lord, your joys
 be vast,
but only where land is free my palace stands.
I labor where I love and where I'm worshiped,
where I am the page of myself alone.
My Lord, your staff's too heavy for my hands
and as for armor, what I happen on
I'll wear on my own frame.
My mother never taught
me metal-polishing,
so in your armory I'd simply
waste my time."
The young man answered Kroutagos the Tzar
he spoke leventes-language sweet, girlsweet,
a meadow brightness shining from his face.
But the king turns darkly and his minions frown,
the youth has lost his wits, he's asked for death.
Kroutagos, you jump down from your throne
and standing face to face you
kiss the young man's brow
and speak virilities:
" Back home now to your friends and mother,
rejoicing in your youth, your gracedeep
 fearlessness.

Remembering; I said
I am the lion himself, though you be of the lion."
When ocean wildens, storm climbs up
and the boat goes wild and dryland
and the men aboard collect themselves
on a lonely raft
that rides and smashes night and day
eaten by endless blackened water's desolation
and suddenly, astoundingly they see white
sails that tremble, open, come, come near,
their drunken joy, their waving woven hands,
their sense of victory
are less than what
the boy brought back,
in conquest to the jubilant crowd.
A bird was noticed from a hidden tree,
was heard to sing this joyful language,
in the key of man, unlike a bird:
" Yesterday while I was sweet asleep
what did I see in dream?
I saw the city's holy place, the mighty palace,
a tree that grew in the palace yard
a cypress tree with golden boughs and golden
leaves and roots and peak,
and on its upmost branches sat
a proud leventes;
health and luck my boy, the widow's pride
and son!

Now East be proud, be jealous, West;
and you, most Holy City, don feasting clothes.
The seed of Makedon is blossom, fruits,
spreads shoots and lesser shoots of kingship,
and of them one the finest growth.
The widow's son.
The Goldengate swings open waiting
now for kings to cross her in their golden crowns.
Turn back to earth and hide inside
it shameful
Bulgarians, Sarakens, and you
from Normandy or Russia."

FIRST WORD

The City! see it there, beyond there on the epic
  field!
And see him too! Raising the crossfirm labarum,
that unjust killer of a gentle kingson,
and himself avenger-handed at destiny's will
the son of the motherland, land
  Frankish-trodden,
the son now here!
The great king of the East, the City's heir
has set his camp and tent at Galata;
his tent is candid, plumed eagle-feather red.
Around him straits and islands, ports, and lands
and towns that know him well,
that know his every word, support him well,
in armored Europe and in fortressed Asia.
They fly to hear his name, they tremble to
  hear his name,
until that noble hour they can blaze that name
his name with a bolt of fire; in East, in West.
Paleologos here, and there, partout, That Name.
And the outspread shores so close so close
in the land that pours and flows and stands
that forested, waveheld, florid, dewy land
which advances with dancing, festivals,
life in the embrace of foster nature

which spends forever and never spares;
the shores that stand as though
prepared to wed—
to mirror themselves in each other's eyes
with love—
today as though reproached, as though dissuaded
watch, dreading the Emperor's mere name.
The City! Look! Beyond there on the field,
  the field
that is mainland broad, and open,
and ravaged, deserted,
and locks in Romany's chief glory,
gloire des rois, of raw or brilliant kings;
kings who lived with swords outside their
  scabbards;
kings—another breed—who wandered in
  meditation,
in mantic aberrations, or science
of the open eyes and grounded feet;
of kings who were never far from Evil,
that whore thicklipped, lowbrowed;
no farther than nail from flesh.
Romany's fame is going, ages, dies though it
  gives
off still an autumn sweetness, bitter laughter
of winter.
Losses, losses, losses, all are lost,
the Field itself is lost, and from the Charse Gate,

down to the Holy Mamas,
to the harbor,
all of the forts are silent, all the tribunals,
the church of John Forerunner, the Palace of
 Seven
no more the sounds of hymns and alleluias
sent to tame the wrath of the All Powerful.
No longer they praise the king, his ascent to
 throne.
Now all is empty; povertied monkly vestige
in the church of John Theologian,
a ruin of buildings,
sheep-pen now for woolly sheep;
and a ruin the sheep-pen too,
the whole a wilderness and desolation.
And deep within the ruins, set far aside,
corrupted, flesh-eaten, hard-to-distinguish,
leavings—as though from crosses; air—as
 though from tombs.
What do you want here, lovers of pleasure:
 you tread
this earth and dankness and stir a stench.
Till yesteryear the stench was
Byzantine ikons, well-set, made with plumb-line
pearl, and mosaic stones.
But Time, that Crapper, made the change
and broke them to bits, ikonoklast,
Isaurian.

Then one spring dawned, poured on the fair
 creation,
the gulfs, the Bosporos, on all the shores
like the purple of some Augusta
on an air-sprite's form.
Then one spring dawned from some strange will
from some strange levity of fate; officers
took whim a light thought waking in them,
the thought of destruction failed an instant
in them
companions to Logothete, the King's adherents,
swordmen, men-at-arms, and sergeants, colonels,
footsoldiers came and infantry,
and stopped beside the ruins. And the place
was groaning with talk and shouts, camaraderie;
and leapings around and songs,
and bursts of festival, of joy.
And suddenly within,
in some mysterious moment, rich, incredible,
a youthful clean-eyed swordman
went out and found himself
face to face with a startling visage
and cast a shrillscream voice.
The others running came.
And see.
Against the battered wall, and nailed—it
 seemed—
into the side of a tomb unsealed, defiled:

against it something
sprung at first from man, converting now to
skeleton; it showed in black upon its bones
a flesh of worms, a
body's final crud.
Entire. Black and naked,
huge, incomparable.
No clothing remained; it only held,
in the hole that was its mouth,
a flute.
He seemed to stand upright, to strain to open,
through a new world's gate, the strangest vision;
to bring it near, and make it part,
he seemed to strain to be the flute's performer,
to draw around it, near it, swordmen, soldiers,
colonels, servants, generals, leaders,
companions of the Logothete, the King's
  supporters
in swiftfoot dance, in dance
led by demons.
And the vision changed, turned to misery; a
  dread,
religious dread has frozen the weird procession
and all before the image, a flock
whom the not yet understood
has bound stockstill in shadows.
Commanders, dukes, and captains,
soldiers, swordbearers, the Logothete himself.

And on the opened, emptied tomb
the carved, half rubbed-out words:
" Kings of the City, your tombs built elsewhere,
hatcheted finer than palaces from marble
with thousand colored marble
of thousand kinds,
brought from Prokonesos, Bithynia,
the quarries of Karystos, and Paros stonemines.
But I, Porphyrogenitos, prouder than all of you
chose here this monastery in the Field,
the poor, untrodden site; and look at me!
I station here and rest; here and sleep.
From the hour when God first called me
to the throne
I knew no rest, I knew no sleep.
The long sword in my hand, no man
found motionless or warless.
My son was war, my daughter victory in war.
Just ask Ismaelites, the Abasgon, the Persian;
just let the Saraken, or better still the Skythian,
supply details."
And a pounding pounded in all their depths
and in their souls a voice, and it repeating:
" Soldiers and swordbearers, sergentes,
tourmarchs,
companions of Logothete, King's officials,
farewell, be well,
be wretched, you who drove the stranger off.

Bitter the vision, yet the outlook good.
Before you stands the Autokrat, the Despot there,
himself complete and uncorrupt, and un-
condemned, and un-
struck down by godly wrath.
Enmarbled king, father and thaumaturge,
an uncorrupt, a holy vestige, brought
again to life,
a thriceblessed presage, angel of the Lord.
Now speak, adore him now, and take
the grotesque, god-breathed flute
out of his mouth
and wash his face with flowered water
and bathe his feet with oily myrrh
send messengers at once to bear
this message to Paleologos
to run and bid him bring
his finest Persian cloths from Bagdad,
Venetian gold, the silk of Thebes,
flowers from the East, and Syrian myrrh,
and funeral clothes, and royal windsheets
for a second funeral, finer than number one.
And since the City is a tattered cloak, whore
of the Frenchman, Italian's slave, and
Spaniard's toy,
remove this hero from the Frank-crossed lands,
to one of the lands of freedom,

some church of Byzance, to
Hellenic lightful land,
go off with him you cavaliers, this
cavalier of all the world,
and open a double thickwalled tomb,
and hammer bronze and steel, and carve
in granite, laying it for him to sleep
again, and whisper over:
" Sleep again, remains, and help us to find,
although you sleep, to find our fatherland again,
while you make search for your third tomb,
your finer tomb, in the purged white City."
And they fell forward, worshiped the wellkept
vestige,
sent messengers to Paleologue.
And the Logothete was silent and went to put
his hand on the skeleton, and take
that playing flute from that playing mouth;
he could not near his hand to touch the flute;
uncanny sounding wraps them all, still
greater mystery. The flute goes on
with speaking, telling; they all ears.
An infinite enchantment poured, as though
the world and all it was had turned to silence
on all sides, and all had changed,
become a single mouth, its voice, the song
they wove.

And thus the voice resounded, the Flute
outspoke:
" Myself the flute, the epic, prophet's reed.
A sistered twin to Klio; my tongue Kalliope.
Sibyl's glance gave me the uncanny eye
Kassandra's shrieking shrieks still in my entrails.
With Hekabe I groaned and heard the mythic
Gorgon's question to the ships:
' Does Alexander live? ' And I, the answer,
answered:
' Lady, Alexander lives and arms, forever one
of us! '
I played and danced Maximo's dance;
I told Akritas' manhood, and spread it
deathless in rumor
to all the ages. And all the Fates have fated me.
First star of the Athenian sky.
I passed by Rome and spread my rooting in the
City.
Eurotas, like a swan you bathed me, and the
rhodo-
daphnes followed, psalming with me.
And I was bathed in Kydnos
shining still the brilliance from Kleopatra.
My wombhomes were the mystical and dreadful
mothers.
A flute my tongue and visage, though I take
on countless visages, and what

I sing is prophecy, and law itself my music.
With wings of dream I fly without support
I soar over the years over the lands;
my ship, my ocean's demon, Fancy.
I turn to trumpet, trumpet over tombs,
awake the dead, put music on their way
and grant the body of the present to the past
and bear you and the future with your offspring
there before you.
The other world is my beginning,
this world my end.
I fill the air with sound; they hear, their ears
  rejoice,
and from that sound I pass on into light
and never stand,
and turn my music to painting, my soul to prosody,
become the bird that twitters human twittertones
and superhuman twittertones. Just hear me
  now, just hear.
No trembling. I am boldness, part of the entire
  world,
I am the lovely countrygirl, girl whom all
have praised.
What callow country boy, or Gallic rube
what crafty North Italian, Romandom's foe,
what evil, sharp young atheist
tell me what ghoulish monster, hoary,
  loathsome, weird,

striking the portal of your inmost nook,
revealing, opening your tomb and plundering,
what thing has smitten, waked you; fouler
of all that's holy; you august? Such is that one
who found me, a reed, upon some bank
and took me, stuck me inside your mouth,
bringing
scorn and unholiness, an utterly blasphemous
laughter.
So that in your teeth I turned to ghost, and am
that still.
But it is you who gave up the ghost, though
before
you gave it, leaped to your horse, you ever
horseman,
and showed yourself to the army shaken
and seething at news of your deathbed hour.
And your favorite pallikars and high-ranked
generals
trembled before your soldiers
for them they could not compass or manage
as you yourself controlled them, managed them.
They only needed to hear your destruction
for you staggered whipped by bitter illness
and reason's light went out in them,
and hope intoxicated them
that they might be your heirs, partake from you
of arms, your victories, your wealth.

You fought with your death.
And were suddenly strengthened.
And it is you, uncanny cavalier, who appeared
to your people
then just before your death turned to Death
himself
froze your dreading people.
And now the very larvae despise you,
the pit shows its scorn.
But I, the flute of laughter and scorn
pronounce my huge pronouncement upon your
lips,
and start and leap and tell the world my song.
I shape a history again, I put you back to life,
City, whom god protects,
together with you, its king,
whose skeleton frame I fill with green and life
and from your battered mouth
I trumpet enormous trumpetings, become
in you a thing more brilliant
than your own true brilliance.
See! In your left hand stands a sword
in your right a lance
on your head a raying brilliant crown,
and snowwhite beard, to form your hieratic
glance,
to be its wreath.
Full and broad your body,

triplethick your chest, and swift your seeing,
like a comet.
And more swift your will.
Your blouseplate goldenwoven,
your chestiron of ruby,
your speech of ruby
your thought of steel,
where you go your road a blast of golden light,
your shoulders castle-towers,
the coat hangs down to your knees plumpurple
bright
and the slippers upon your feet are red
and you shine from feet to skull and watch
advancing before you enslaved, ambassadors
of nations you brought to subjugation.
Above your head Akrites of the sky
in manliness and saintliness
as pilgrims for the cross,
the two Theodori,
one a commander the other soldier,
and the cavalier who slew the dragon,
and the hero thaumaturge from Saloniki,
those double growths whom
only their horses divided,
the Saint Demetrios on a roan,
the Holy George on a cream.
And up there higher messengers, archangels
eminent,

they fly in jealousy, approach your armor,
and over them, unreachable, the king of all,
king who holds wreaths of the just for your
  reward.
You King of Romany, you servant of Christ.
O Lord! The sky of Fancy, historical world,
though filled with image of You;
yet nothing will last for eyes of men,
no idol, painting, or weft; nor shadow
from all your palaces, all your temples,
from all your golden dining couches,
from all those rooms
worked by master artists with mastery
on wall, mosaic, tapestry, stone.
Yet far more than your image or statue
I, your flute, will raise you a hymn
to the end of time."

SECOND WORD

Those lovely islands, tragic islands, nine
solitary islands.
With verdant Prinkipo and naked Prote
in the arms of Marmara they close their ranks
like chains,
these miracles of green, these miracles of white,
jewels of the straits, workshops of destruction,
they drip with honey, dew, with light, with
myrrh with blood.
Mysterious, mystical, mute and grave they are.
And with the grace of roses, with the pallid
evening,
at times when, counter to every logic, certain
sounds
that fill with silence, sounds unheard by any
daytime ear;
the day so laboring with heavy sounds
that fill the mind,
at times when certain sounds slip through the
air and weave,
susurring, then those who fall to shadow easily
or those whom something in air will brush,
are moved at the hearing.
And these are sounds,
emerging from those islands' inner depths,

those tragic islands,
as though from drowned and swirling worlds,
are sounds that rise, spread. Are bells,
and call to matins, vespers, vigils;
forgettings of the world,
and prayer, perfuming waft of thought, ascends
with them.
Shouts break the air, rendings,
and flesh is torn, and bones—it seems—are
shattered,
curses descend, darken the skies, and go.
Here in the waters of Marmara, the gardens of
its azure,
where planters are nereids and harvesters sirens,
the clefts and cells and sketes
bend, are mirrored, tremble; holding
the innocent and evil in the torture of exile.
Here the nesting homes of Grace, the haunts of
Death.
And the psalming of monks and the striking of
their bells,
go forth to the bitter corpses, lives still bitterer.
And scepters! Look! In ruins! Look! And
crowns! Mere jokes!
And you the pillars of forts, commanders of
palaces,
princes born to the purple, lions of battle,
you who handled love as toy in one

fair hand, and in the other hand
the State, another toy; you haughty queens!
And so the scales of chance go up and down.
Now ruined, pallid, naked, abandoned
to shirts of hair, to winding-cloths for habit.
And if your eyes have not been plunged
by the executioner's sword
into dawnless night,
your tearless eyes, your tear outflooding eyes,
your supplicatory, hopeless eyes
in vain sometimes you fasten their glance
  toward the City,
which before you endlessly gleams and speaks
  its blackness,
or sometimes toward that point
toward the Bithynian mountains and coasts
which nod you farther, aery, joyous.

On those lovely islands, tragic islands, nine
  solitary islands.

Mauve is the rosemary, yellow the wheat,
a bursting, a rising anew of rosemary and wheat.
And May the luxurious king weaves with the
  Moon
felt unfulfilled and drunken loves

drunk with endless birdsong,
songs of the coasts of Thrace,
those singing sleepless coasts that sun,
the sun of Anatolia, burns hard and lives.
Felt unfulfilled and drunken loves,
drunk from the all-harmonic pieces played
for that ardent king of May that he
might have joy in that lovely child the Moon;
in the mastic trees and myrtles, arbutus, black-
berry,
crabapples, holmoaks, thick-woven pines
whose covering caresses, whose breath is balsam,
have joy in whatever greenly sings in silence,
blooms, gives shadow, stirs.
Within this sweetkissed greenness
which shields against highnoon seizing heat,
see Prote! That desiccated cliff,
as though bathed by the blood of a wound
that drips, will never close, for years.
And opposite the Golden City, the " Heavenly
City,"
as the ancient singer had called it,
place apart though in the midst,
though lacking for green, yet living
rejoiced in the sea's embrace
and in the sky's; and there across
always the brilliant Bithynian Olympos,
realm of the ascetes;

rosewhite in dawn and evening, always snowed,
an ecstatic soul which always,
to purify the world,
accepts the failings of the world.
Prote, triple convent, with monasteries three,
and in the maul of the wolf destruction, three
famous kings who lived and died,
the doomed, the abandoned, and the tortured,
yet still intact, locked into tombs, and
  uncorrupted
and turned to shades; they return at night, are
wildbeasts of the underworld,
and before them the fearless tremble like stags.
Then the island's winding narrow paths,
serpents along the beach, along the peaks,
inscribed in cramping bends, well know,
and all of the island's corners know.
And the ruling kings are triple, Rangabes,
the seductive Lekapenos, and unequalled
Diogenes the Greek.
The first lived humbly, passed from the sun
to total night in peacefulness, holding till
the hour of death, as ever, his vision nailed
to the sight of the holy distant palace
sunfire playing, calling forever.
The second—speak yourself, who at his call
you monks, monastics, hermits, black
of blackest troops, you swarthy cloud, black lives

were driven here to this bare island
from groveling cells, from sea-
coasts of Bithynia and from
the wooded stones around Olympos
from the giant ascete monastery
summit of ridge of pure Axentios,
and from the shores of Bosporos made holy
by those images of mystic prayer, the stylites.
Speak up who saw that favorite of fame,
halfnaked, kneeling, rent and torn,
who saw him weep, whip himself before you
confessing his sinner faults
while an instructed boy, with whip,
attacked and insulted his flesh to blood.
And his name made history. Address
with your chorus' heavy refrain: Take pity, Lord!
Eleison, Kyrie!
And third the incomparable, a favorite of fame,
the governor fearless, the Kappadokian great one,
Halepi's polemarch, the lord of Adana.
A dike he was to Togroul, the cataract,
and held back Arpaslan, the Turkish Sultan,
who, windblown cavalier from Pontic Mountains,
Armenian passes, poured down to plains
of Antioch. And later! Look! The Sultan's slave
he became
and later, the lamentable slave, servant
in the nation he'd ruled; the one who ate scorn,

was whipped like a mule, was spat upon
by any Jew, was driven out
and from hands that had perfumed him with
incense
and lighted candles for him, had
beating, torture, knouts and blinding at last.
Unshaken, holding fast, a martyr
in the arms of a queen
queen who knew him not
when his power thundered
and his sword was lightning;
her unpredictable soul, weird female heart—
she pitied him later, when his body
was laughable, shameful version of what it had
been
a wounded and miserable man, a castoff,
she came, stood beside,
and closed his dying eyes,
while over them enormous birdwings beat,
and ravens croaked and deathbirds circled.
The eyes of Diogenes Romanos were closed
on that red island, on its highest summit,
his war-delighting soul flew off
to find new mainlands, oceans, west and east.
To become a rooting in the land, a storm at sea!

On those tragic islands, those lovely islands,
those lonely islands.

And now the Empress! Look! In the Athenian
sun
that flower born of longing and death,
that maga of men, careful, wise,
harsh Athenaia,
who ruined her womb's own fruit
is now the island's offal, its horror,
she who was mother of her people
not one to weep at her own fate.
Her hopelessness a stone.
She drags round the shore like a reef,
a black lamia of the shore.
Stay far, stay far, all ships!
Now take her, ocean, with debris, debris.

But who will speak with *you*, and who divine you,
Empress, young as a goddess,
who separate, unreconciled, alone
grow drunk with vision,
advance through astral loneliness?
Who with a drawing pen would dare to try
a portrait worthy of you;
what flute attempt to fill with your enormous
song
and not be burst to pieces?
Who unastonished could aspire to whiff

that snowstill lily, or drink its potent fragrance,
to drink in sleep and death together
thing infinitely sweet, insatiably desired on earth?
And see *her* now, that Spartan one! I know not
whether Sparta bore her
or is the thought that
grew her and raised her.
I only know she watered in those waters
that watered ancient Helen
among kissing reeds, among cygnet longings.
I know not if her birth was in some wretched shop
or if she saw first light
in aristocracy's gold crib.
I know the frightful birthless Mothers
who live apart from time apart from place
controlling in chasms of embrace
all forms deserving life, which do not die,
these forms all beautiful, these unseized dreams of
  world
that certain magicians can bring us again
I know these unimaginable Mothers
granted her the grace of Helen's grace.

But now! Look there!
Augusta Theophano! Grace and Fury! Look!
She holds a wand, a delicate wand
on its crest a threeleaved golden lotos.

It is the lotos you can never eat
the poisonous aconite which
at sight debilitates
that melts you at touch,
whoever you are, roué, ascetic,
all is at once forgotten; life and power, youth,
and—if you be a man of honor—honor,
throne—if you are king,
high bourgeois, you turn to beggar, hermit,
infant for her love, and murderer for her kiss.
And with her wand she rules and binds the
  polemarchs,
their reasoning their hearts, their worlds their
  people:
The Emperors, the Romans, Tsimiskides,
  Phokades,
and all which they, who are ruled or bound,
transport on the ships of sea, the camps on land,
the naked swords and the strong young men
and the bitter fire that burns,
destroys—and does not go out.
And like that fire that extinguishes not,
in the sea, itself,
that ruins and judges on land and sea,
like it Augusta Theophano, everywhere, ever ruler,
she rules within the heart, rules within the City.
And like the rainbow her nipples gleam
and from them nurse and tremble at root

the timid, girlish royal child,
and the never beaten victor of emirs;
she gleams, angelic vigil at the heavenly gate
her smile a music on her expressive lips.
Behold Augusta Theophano! She smiles and
  slaughters;
oh how you hang, rare victims, on the tip of her
  wand!
Behold Augusta Theophano! She smiles and drips
the blood of murder and destruction, as dawn
  drips
through ruddy pearls of dew.
Audacious to youth, debauch to the old,
she bends the unbendable, takes down the stars.
With her own beauty like a golden scythe
her thought a spider, opiate her love.
Ragess and sphinx, you flesh, you serpent, you
  Aphrodite!

Unbent, unruined, the queen of all, but darkly,
shadow from some all-brilliant day, she makes
sheer cliffs a paradise, the night a dawn,
and bears each other shadow to her feet,
and makes it, before her, to shine like moon
whose body's light is from her sun.
And opposite her, kneed to ground, the other
  masters,

three, Anatolian dukes,
the minions of the dame
who ate them when hungry, who drank them
when thirsty,
yet had never enough of these
visions from somewhere outside life, from outre
tombes
held only (forever) in the enchanting halo
her shadow's shadow spread,
those three who address and groan,
Romanos, Phokas, and the third Tsimiskes,
one by one, all three, and that one lady.
And they remark:
" Alembic of attar of roses, perfume of
Alexandria,
cup with purple lips, cup filled with longing!
Festive, hunter, prowler through night, chevalier
for just one taste, one kiss, for all
the sweetnesses of love, its madness, brilliance,
emptiness.
My throne was always love, my crown was
pleasure
and of my youth's derangement, people, you
were the comrades.
Unknown to those who ruled, the captain's foe,
the first into the circus, and king to every whore.
My minister of state a pimp, a palace fool my
admiral.

The gardens of the Holy Palace know me,
with roses I crown my impure capers
harbors, moles, and fields, and castles know me
how I go running after partridge, startle deer,
and with golden traps go catching girls.
In shadows of century-old oaks
the Anatolian shores or Chalcidian forests
in frequent greeting have watched me turn
my pack of hounds in chase of the boar.
But in one dawn when I was going to hunt,
alone, some slippery prey, I went
my way into a cleft's deep core
and entering a cave I met
you, queen, by accident;
we spoke.
You slaved me then. You put me low.
Your child, you ordered me.
My world is in your flesh, my fire your eyes.
One night in bed with you is worth
a victory at arms.
You speak? You harvest hearts. You laugh?
Destruction of wills.
A spell your beauty, a suffocation your arms,
your power unpitying, tigerstrong your decision.
You ruin with the sword, or dissolve with potions.
From Prousa I returned to see
my noble father, ruined with aging
in the golden gallery.

The queen, my honored mother, I placed
living buried in a monastery.
Just for you.
And all my precious sisters, hugely loved
(Zoe, Theodora, Theophano, those darlings,
Anna, Agatha)
I wrote them out of life, robbed them of youth;
a whipping of those flowered bodies;
the habit of a nun,
and I chopped off from each, rich
splendid hair, its silky gracious flowing,
and laid it on your altar, sacrifice
to your insatiable passion.
And my own life, itself a churn of pains
I brought to you. You drank it down. It's gone.
What next?"

" I want that gloomy hero whose life's half done,
is middle-aged; who goes in heaviness,
a darkened face and bent, loose-ends,
forever on age's sill, yet not quite there.
I want the hero who gave his people
—toys to children—splendid portals,
marvels of enamel, of ivory,
from the Thasian castles and from Mopsuestia;
the ascetic hero knowing all conversions
in his strictness, knowing

nothing of a woman's body, remaining pure,
an unshaped column, granite
rooted somewhere on the ocean's coast,
column smoothed never by an artist's hand,
yet the wave delights to batter it
whipping its heavy burden with smoothing foam,
like some great mass it longs to weather,
mass which the ship loves to bind to itself,
fastening its prow to that as yoke.
I long, myself the ivy, to choke him,
myself the rumbling earth to quake
him, hero pleasure-hating, creature ugly;
my fancy shapes him like a cedar
high on Tauros, among lovely and countless
  cedars,
standing higher than the firs, higher than the
  pines. O come!"
"I've come. Phokas. Victor of all except you!
My mistress, queen of love, ruler of all my
  longing,
You rule all loves, now give me longing.
An Hagion Oros skete suits me
better than Augustus' crown;
before the glory that grows and gleams
on the brow of Portaitissa Lady
I scorn the glory of throne and fete.
But you I saw, and to deserve you turned
  Emperor!

Put my crown before your feet, my mind in your
bondage.
Old and jealous am I. The traps of manhood,
the world's seductions—though fearless I am—
I tremble at these.
I seized you, closed you and my jealousy
and my outlaw longings in the giant
Boukolean castle-palace, built sheerly over wave,
with triple, fourfold lofty unreached walls.
And through the savage midnight's voice,
that maddened voice, that warning voice of
heaven and hell,
which hoarsely shrieked: ' In vain, my Lord,
you raise
the triple, fourfold lofty palace walls.
Construct them high as heaven, and bar all
gates;
misfortune will find you, Justice strike you! '
And toward that savage midnight's prophet voice
I groaned, replying: ' Spirit, I have no fear.'
I fell down then and slept upon the lionskin;
the lion less savage than your passion.
And me you slaughtered with Tsimiskes' sabre.
Now? You want? "

" The other. My first burden, that one—my
final sickness.

For all of you I fancied. That man
that man only
I worshiped.
I want that wide-eyed, easy man;
his eyes are blue and peaceful, draw and drown.
His visage a tallow eros, and in his heart
the song of Holy George is raging,
Digenes' clan are smiting.
I sit, I stand, I walk, I sleep, I cannot sleep,
yet whether I eat or drink, my lord, you are
ever in mind.
You know; you were the tables where I sat
eased,
ate and drank, got drunk and drowsy,
those very tables, in a drowsing time
I pushed away, and overturned with this my
foot
which crushes worlds.
But he is the Holy Table.
And from the hour when I came
into the light of sun, like spirits, insatiable,
I came, as puissant, queen and mistress came
with shiver of lusting in my marrow,
and in embraces forced
the crushing of male.
And on my longing's altar night
and day his flesh is burning,
and dusk and dawn his kiss forever hums.

But one time only for youth, one time for that
spring,
just once you lightninged in my heart's still night,
love for the wanderer,
love for the denier."

But shadow number three, denier, wanderer,
has locked his mouth, and will not open
it for whoever, for any reason.
Mute. A mighty ennui has ruined him,
smashed his teeth, has melted him, drunk him
down.
He wastes like some confounded child, or
fruitless garden,
that hero who terrified Russians,
Edessa, such times on end,
and the places round Ister's feet.
Ennui, ennui . . .
Forever within him it is,
in upper world or in inner shadows,
it eats him, and eating deprives him of voice,
within him distilling something, nameless substance,
substance too bitter to name with sufferings,
too bitter to reveal with sounds.
Because the sword is large that slaughtered his
father,

because the sword is large and great the crime,
because the queen who betrayed him
is greater still.

So on the tragic islands, lonely lovely islands
those queens of loss, those regents of death,
leaving their tombs, take walks, and meet.
They mourn their sufferings and tell them aloud
in the rays of moonlight, in the sweetness of May,
the magics of the evening. Bells; they call
to matins, vespers, the loss of the world:
and groanings clamor, and writhings slash the
air.
And suddenly a sharptoned trumpet, and
poundings of hooves,
a battalion's turmoil, and before it a horseman,
horse and man together; advances,
as if paying obeisance coming, Theophano,
to you
and he too thirsting for your kiss,
that king your Son!

Let others grow angry, and curse
your memory, recoil at your name.
Let others speak out and publish your beauty,
like the flame of fire, the tiger's coat.

Prophetic flute I am, and epic flute.
I raise you a temple, light your torches, hymn
your image in the incensed smoke. Glory,
glory to you, queen Kentauress, mother
who brought the Kentaur king to life,
as in mythrich Hellas was born
by a trident's blow
from bitter waves
that much praised steed.
So in cosmogonic time
some mountain, castle of earth and roof,
was thrown up from a giant pit
by some enormous freeing quake.
The arrow of Love, the sword of war:
two makings hard to distinguish
from that time when they strike hard
or support with strength
the holy and worthless moments
of the soul and life.
Lubricious Love, and violent War,
two horses that whinny impatient, and paw the
ground.
And woman is the mother-fountain; from her
come forth our sin and saving, ascension, Death;
the sword that slaughtered you, my Lord,
Nikephoros,
and the womb that bore you, Bulgarkiller, Lord!

Triple streets, quadruplestreets, and paths.
 That man.
That man is known; to lakes,
ridges, cities, portals, passes, clefts
Bodena, Skoutari, Skopia, Berati
Makedonian forests, all those regions,
the field of Pelagonia, Triaditsa's highway.
Wherever Romaic flesh-consuming arrows
have struck men of other races, and the
 Amalichite.
He smote and slew and took (in slavery)
the Danube Bulgars, Balkan Slavs;
and Boyars and Slavic leaders
with chains around their necks,
with brazen ankle chains, he dragged
dragged like birds and dogs behind,
and dragged, to his wagon tied, your house,
 Tzarina.
And he captured Longokastro, proceeding from
 Longo
to Kastoria which spreads by the lake its
 greenness,
and Samuel's last forces he destroyed
and in the river drowned the filthy Petsenegue,
and burned, beyond near Ostrovo, the palace
 of the Tzar,

and here destroyed and smashed to ground,
and founded there, and brought to life.
And the Bosograda fell, and Bistritsa groaned,
and Vladislav fled and Nikolitses went,
and from Brochotos' summit Daphnomele
dragged bound Ibatse at the ruler's feet.
They came, they worshiped him and handed
over the keys of forty castles
the swords of forty castellans
they came:
Dravomires, the sons of Vladislav, all,
and Bogdanos with Krakras and with Dragomouz,
with Krakras given birth by one
last hero, Rhodope.
In Preslava he stayed, and came from Prespa,
that place set like an island,
like a painting,
against its unforgotten lake, its wooded plains
with giant wooded mountains buttressed.
The Vardar he passed, and Skopia saw him,
and where he went—oblations made,
and where he passed—hymns made.
And knees went slack in genuflection
tears in streams were shed,
and kisses on the ground he trod.
And after Mosunopole Serres,
inlocked by ridges, threw open gates;
he sailed the Strymon to Adrianople,
and all who were not there arrived

and worshiped him,
and gathered soil that he had walked
and bent and tore their heads of hair.
That rider of the plain,
he takes untaken Pernikon,
an eagle nesting in Pronista's tower.
And on to the inaccessible, strange court,
yes on to Ochrid, Bulgar heartland,
standing hidden high: *en face* a magic lakeside
then where the winding Drinos comes
elongate, dark, and blasts
into the Adriatic.
Then he trod Ochrid's treasuries, palaces,
and with its treasures he paid his army,
and Tzarrich crowns of pearl he found
and a hundred of dinars in golden monies
were gathered into his tent
a warp itself of silk and gold.
Nor could Chemara's untrodden place,
Tmoros on highstraight peak, that roughest
  ridge,
nor could Tmoros survive to leave
untouched, unslaved,
from the race of Simeon, of Sischman,
a hand for off-warding, a foot for fleeing.
They saw him, knew him and forget him never,
for everywhere he broke his lightning-sudden
  path

whatever huge blockade or
giant plains made obstacle,
the Kaukasos, the Nile, the Apennines,
the Tauros and the Antitauros.
And from the Sava to the Winter Mountains,
all his own monocracy
up to the Balkans.
The Black Sea hears him, its ices melt . . .
the golden Adriatic feels
sometimes his shadow
a spreading through air and storm.
From Thrace he moves, appears in the City.
And takes his further élan toward Antioch
to find the Saraken, and is not held
by swampyland or snow in the Syrian mountains.
And in his nearness all lose fear
of sickness, failure, fear itself; tant
pis for the tired who pray, the fallen's cries.
Forever forward. Enough for him,
whether many or few, those men
the chosen, elect, as many as last;
endure;
they have in their lungs the breath of his own air.
On every side of him the caliphs
light the fire
and their villages flame, and they drop their
  weapons,
and run toward Damascos, Lebanon's shelter,

saving their skins from the moment they heard
his horse's hoofclacks, clacks of destruction.
The emirs bend and bow to the ground
and drag their heads in the dust for pity.
From Armenian mountains down to the shores
of Italy fame bore his name and ran with it;
it sailed the Danube in dawn and went at evening
surging forth and cleansed in pure Euphrates.
And above them all, his fame went over the land
whose jewel is Pangeon,
Thessalonike
its queen, and Edessa its fountainmother,
that land the Slavic dream, Romaic curse.
That country spreads and ripens, and flowers out
and strides between Axios, Aliakmon,
where those mad rivers, Vardari, Vistritsa,
cease never, but flow their banks and rage, and
race,
and guard the land and liven
the land;
but vainly.
For floodings of people, a deluge of nations
surge forever the land and flood the land;
some civilized, some barbarous, some old,
some modern—
both nothing men and men of note cross swiftly,
deftly, searching here, exploring there,
and strike, and wait,

as though all searched in this earth
a giant statue
hatcheted out of gold,
a form which once stood straight, and startled
on Slatovreki mountain,
a high peak of that mountain.
They fight to find the statue, and find it not,
but vision amazes them, and the very country
stands
like amazing vision, phantasy-breeding.
Above all toward this country goes his fame,
fame nomad, yet here at home
his fame now hawk, and eagle, falcon, all,
his fame has now turned to heron, now fisher,
to eat that uneaten locust the Bulgar.

When bravely he'd fought that glorious fight
he stopped. A rest? But never!
For that driver of armies one thought
forever advancing, a drive to the road.
Forever.
In his military breastpiece
beneath the gold beneath the iron
beneath his weapons, beneath his flesh,
the acrid hairshirt's bite,
he feels it like penitent ascete:

he wears it; his body whips him, leaving him
helpless,
preserving, for all his whipping, his bitter,
fasting,
tortured and satan-trusting flesh.
And sometimes he feels in his heart
as if with fingers, feeling, palping,
the ikoned image of Mary seems to turn blood
for him,
of Mary protectress whose image forever
he wears on his breast for relic,
held as he was in the grace of Mary.
He stopped; he thought; he longed to place
a last jewel to his crown, which shone with
jeweled
spoils of war and wildness, longed to cast
the shining pearl of feeling, prayer.
And what was most upon his mind?
His God? The final judgment? The realm of
Heaven?
The glory of the Greeks? Man's history?
Salvation? Race? His soul?
Who knows? The clouds across his mind were
torn
apart by certain queens, nursers of nations,
certain lands,
and they shone before him, each in its form.

Between the Tiber and the Flaminian Way,
upon the Campus Martius we see the rent and
  pitiable
queen of all, still Rome, and on her body
walk, conversing, Pope and Caesar.
And you, the White Sea's jewel, Alexander's
  city:
constant to the Jewish merchant, purlieu of the
  Arab,
you, asleep, while on you falls the Nile
in power, and makes you pregnant,
you, in sleep, Hellenic queen, and in your dream
the beauty of Hypatia, the gold of India.
Holy Sion, handed over to
the cruel Fatimite, his harem,
Sion heart of Palestine
yearns distantly from its castle's tower
into the pass across, to the shore above,
and to the sea;
and, crucifier of the Savior, waits for its own
  salvation.
And Antioch shines, beside Orontes, virgin,
a field with flowers, a sky with stars.
And Pergamon hidden in its inbound bay
dreams of its war-delighting gods

dreams of its giants,
and with a sorcered mirror
with Augusta's purple
see! Armida, Lady!
Above them all!
And far apart, aside, as if in scorn,
Athens
bright with sun, and fair with sun,
in labor and poverty
extending her hand for help
yet hopeless
with her head upright,
her broadened forehead deep
in thought and greatness,
peaceful forehead, bare, as though awaiting
hand, to give it once again
the diamondskill of Craft.
The victor, the barbarian who sought
some concord, shade for coolness, cove for rest,
the victor, Rome, did not remain in you,
did not go forth to hold you, City, joyful,
nor did he stay in you, Jerusalem,
nor in you, Bithynian queen
with twiceahundred towers,
Nikaia! Nor in Makedon's Thessalonike
revealed against the Seven Mountain,
like some patrician Zoste at Augusta's flank.
And not in your enormous home

of prayer and Christendom,
Chalcidian Holy Mountain,
burning ever incense
night and day ascension.
Pergamon and Antioch and Alexandria:
of these not one;
Athens, you he loved.
To you he went.

In Seven Mountain's city upon the walls
Vlacherniotissa is moving, more strong than walls,
and takes their measure,
and terrifies in her going
air and stars above and earth and sea around.
Like archangelic sword she clutches
in her faultless hands
the lightning-winged miraculous cloak, maphori,
ready always to plunge its border
in the Narrow's wave
to waken winds, to untie tempests,
that they might once and forever swallow
the Avar, Bulgar, Arab, Russian,
whoever will come as foe
with ships or skiffs
against the land the Virgin guards.
There where Athos stations,
that vigil Taxiarch which guards

the Makedonian paradise, its gate,
that crown of monasteries, roof of Holy Mountain
that—behold her!—Portaitissa!
And on *her* lap the Word
an infant.
And in the Virgin's eyes—a world,
a heaven of heart and love—a world,
from Eden's lilies to the grapples of Hell.
If she but stir her hand, all be blessed,
the rich, the poor, the just, the evil; from the cicada
to the plain of the jeweled and outspread ocean
outspread around her feet; it she holied
when from Nikaia she came to the shore, a
marvel, glory,
fiery column, choreographer of foam and wave.
But the conqueror, barbare, does not
repose his thought on her, Vlacherniotissa,
nor on the glories of Iviron.
The Mistress of the Skies he goes
to worship where she built
her castle on Athena's rock
and from all the compass points,
from all high Thule
takes holy offering, the faithfuls' vow,
and she follows that Athena
who is joy in war
yet with her same ebullience, her selfsame air,
but joyful in peace, without shield or sword.

For victory, her hands are swords, are shields,
and before her faultless breast
Medusa's dreadful head is harmless
before that matterless bosom's image
that depicts the Christ, an allsweet child.

1018. Backward, forward, chant and come,
sing, you strange flute you ghostly tongue,
in the mouth of the specter
which in very coming is shout
that if fame is smoke, fame is also a cliff.
You can no longer tell, who see him so;
scarecrow, absurd; is he still That One?
You cannot say he is someone else
for there as you see him you worship his name
fall down and worship. I am the flute, the one,
who rests in the lips of the specter who bears
us news of the lower world, sent
from the darkness of the abyss,
who lives his life more fully
more bathed in light
than men who rejoice their lives in the sun.
I that strange strange flute
who sanctify my purposes
breathe a sibyl air, turn prophetess
a beauty with beauty of all the ages;
who bring the distant near, untomb the buried,

return its meaning to the meaningless;
uncoverer of what
tomorrow brings;
a speaker of the unknown sound
the wise sounds which burst out
astonishing, and never heard before;
and astonish you;
all good and true and lovely things I love
rejoice in them, salute them, fight
that you too love, salute
extraordinarily
and love
above them all, beyond them all,
the bestborn good.
I give you
Athens.

Are you the one who wears that Mesa for crown?
The Mesa who supports that temple,
crown of crowns?
Temple,
temple who made you
beauty prime inter pares
and for Ever
you of every grace?
In you revelations:
rhythm, each line a Muse;

Word your marble has become
and your conception art
and you have come in thaumaturgic land
which meditates this all
with aid of Horae, measured Horae;
above these people, above these people's faiths,
you came
Cyclopean, limber, as though a painting.
Like infinitely precious cloths
the same in dryness or dampness, light or
  darkness,
which hand has never woven,
which time cannot destroy
nor eye perceive beginning,
whence it was
and no man's mastery of art
can start this work again,
for what it is was worked from dew
by nereids with foam
by angelhands with rays of light.
Thus you! Nor could you elsewhere, temple,
  have lived,
than where you first took growth.
Flower, and Athens your vase.
Here once the well of deathlessness;
now desolate weeping.
On this very soil, in the land of your own gods,
as from deathless ones the tears

took root and blossomed
and blood from heroes
dripped to the soil below
and sustained their race
so you rooted and grew
narcissi, hyacinths, anemones, daphnes
and all that passed in form from man to flower.
And wherever they took growth from you
stole seed from you,
came forth uneven growth
or growthless seed.
Temple, your foundations are not rooted
as if, immense in depth,
they reached to the world's still quick,
nor does your brow advance
beyond the clouds
like colossal pyramid
in Africa's desert.
Olympian hands
maintain you double lightly
in bright diaphanies of air.
No rash transcending in your ascent
or loss in measurelessness
where the eye is foiled:
you gently draw and bear
the spirit to those regions.
No hordes of slaves established you,
no manshaped cattle spurred
by loveless, blood-consuming tyrants.

You they raised with reason
yes with song:
in reasonings where Law
gave birth to Polity,
came into birth with rhythm,
was itself song;
and your subduer, marble, temple,
your first former,
a conqueror without struggle,
without struggle a shaper.
And hear! Whenever a man wants
access to his youth again, he comes
to Beauty's fountain, washes.
There in facing all these beauties
stands disinterested and bends in feeling
suppliant, lover, singer, passer.
When he has offered to all, acquired from all,
over and over to You
may he return in hymn.
That the world's renewal might begin with you,
with you find ending.
Where shall I find, and if I find
how shall I understand your beauty's soul,
my temple, or drink from that soul's mystery?
What fingers, hands, will play it out for me,
what breath unfold
your mystery in me like rose-red blood
that I may make it chant
a chant worth you?

Spears, stoneheave weapons, " scorpions,"
slings, and battering rams.
Give way, thrust of the axe, cast of the bow.
The hags of the earth are atremble
the ocean gorgons tremble
at the magic fire.
A Scylla from the abyss,
a hellspent fury,
ruins, camps, and fortresses—magicianness.
Minotaurs, lampreys, vipers; all savage game at
once
is this wild fire!
The archangelic guide of Constantine flew down
and New Rome sprouted up.
And in the doublewidth
of his bright wing
he held this wingswift fire.
To that great king
yet greater gracing:
in one swiftsilent lightwinged glance
with one hand gave The City
with the other
mystic fire.
A fire:
the vigil guardian of the mainland,

destroyer on high seas
from caves in the Morea to Euphrates
lightener of night, a storm by day,
the Nation's fire.
Spears, stoneheave weapons, "scorpions,"
battering rams and slings.
" Coups de hache," the bow's trajectile
a rust on the weapons, the enemies change, and
the ages go, but see! the Fire!
Glory to you the Hellenes
glory to you of The City,
men, real men,
and sons of men.
Romaic leventia;
to the fire of the Greeks
that ruined the Arabs and Russians
the Bulgars and Avars . . .

Listen, from every theme, from their battalions,
the men of the line, leventes platooned,
are chanting the brilliant fire, the savage fire,
a mighty blessing, a mystery mightier,
which sturdies Byzantine blood through the ages.
Their voyaging comes through, the attacks have
ceased,
fighting—evil and sleepless—has reached its end.
They hasten to worship the maiden of Athens

to worship on bended knees
with scabbarded swords; the flags are waving.
Caesars and exarchs, magistri, domestics, and
  dukes,
bowmen, messengers, borderguards, swordsmen,
  sentries,
irregulars, regulars,
lancers, cavalry, infantry
captains, aristocrats, men of the road,
recruited
from the Dodecanese to Iceland.
Vantroops, infantry, panzers, the best of the
  troops,
volunteers, fighters for money,
the mighty's forced laborers, the wind's
  collections,
of every country and race, of every
mind, and heart and tongue,
the fowl of all four poles,
wild beasts of every world,
under single labarum, single rule,
a single dream for their shelter; and you, Idea,
you bind them,
Bosporos City, Constantine's daughter.

But I, the mystic flute, the dreamstruck flute
cannot weave this list with skill

recounting exactly and carving
on my language marble
the actual in its order
these crowds of wanderers, faces of men.
In single phantasy of dream they pass—
a dream which fades upon appearance—
they pass
amazement for the eyes, and for ears a deafening;
I speak, myself, again, and echo, and say again
as though giving some distant music
to the image of my dream.
Like one who passed through quickly, distracted,
with the drive of youth that held
his thought to another point, like one who
passed, when young, through a foreign land,
and who remembers later, suddenly
yet cannot recall this land clear imaged
to paint its form again—for no trace stays—
and through his mind it passes and leaves
him something distant, marvelous, unspeakable—
that foreign land—
yet is ever like foreign face
which was once and somewhere met
and fastened against our eyes
a glance that can never
be rooted out of the heart.
Winds of feeling and lyric storms
are whipping the calm of my epic's sea.

And the boat sails on in the waters
of restless imagination, ever in vision.
And now my ship is filled and armed,
O worshiping autocrat, with you and your forces!

The battalions pass by, advance one by one,
the weapons unsheathed, the armors glittering.
And Hellenic soldiers from everywhere
summoned
from the caves of Taenaros to Haemos passes.
What name do they follow?
And who are they?
And how should I keep them apart?
Men of violence, pell-mell,
and their image
here blurred
extinguished there
outlined on a background of dark;
it slips, grows distant, attempts to return into night.
Kephallenians: bespeaking the worths
of the Seven Islands,
finesouled men.
From musksweet Zakynthos.
Leukadians, armatoloi by training,
heroes of heart.
Fellows from Kerkyra, the City's ally,
City forever bewitched by the stranger,

guarding the hereditary
palace's entrance—
a queen within—
a lithewand guardianess of the gates.
And men from Krete, island that neither
ages nor bows,
that fills with the breath of heroes
and huge ascension
from Krete—enslaved, unslavable—
instructive forever of freedom
watering with native blood
their fatherland's waterless tree
and making it strong.
The Kretans, hawks of the mainland, of ocean,
ever inarmed in iron; in movement, in straight
menvigils upon the mountain, upon the mast.

From the slopes of Fivefingered Mountain, look!
Choleric, arrogant despite great scorn,
respectless of masters
and harsh to their own, as to strangers,
with robbery for Lord, their passion gain,
past masters of ambush;
though Christians, by name,
preserving in fact a spark
of faith in the broken idols,
in ancient Hellas.

The first Greek idols.
A spark in the ashes.
And look! The men of Mani.
Resembling their cliffs, upright and cragged,
naked, untrodden, apart,
cliffs of Kakovounia, of Matapan.
Pirates par excellence.
And with them gather others, gather only with
 them,
others unbent, the last the few
believing in ancient extinguished Olympians,
the eaters of monks.
From the leading lands of Morea
serfs, bourgeois, and leaders
from bulwarks, property, little castles
from little castles perched
like rooted trees
on escarpments
perched not to be taken.
Men from Lakedaimon, still the renowned
the land of towers, noble walls and clefts,
and men from the campwalled quadrate polities
from Korinth, and Argos, Anaplion, Monemvasia.
Blessings, Argolid, soldiers' land,
the land that's rich in all, a seedbed,
bearing womb of pallikars.
Men from Patras which adores its holy cavalier
its Saint Andreas:
with it Korone.

From fortresses to harbor-holding shores
from strengthless forts you can take by sword
from the inaccessibles, the cliffcave fortresses
the great and level mountain-castles
from places in fields
ingirthed with crenelations, towers,
and from Vostitsa's land
from Kalamata the lovely
with waters, sumptuous meadows,
its single castle like a cloister
from the mountains that stand like castles from
nature,
from those that stand like fragments
from strongholds
from the countless castles, keys of their regions,
from clefts and hillocks and woods
lands, and counties,
oblative, borne, these warriors.

And others:
from untouched mountains and from inlocked
camps
holding inheritances pure,
their fathers' giving,
though the ages diminished
it.
And others, the land's own children,
the bodies of men of the open fields.

These enlivens the soul of a foreign breath
a primal soul, a soul of original life
a Latin breath, Vlach breath,
and chiefly a Slavic spirit.
The Hellenic born, Romaics,
Turkseeds—all one faith,
a single tongue, and thought, and soul,
One Race.
Befoulings, blastings of wind, graftings, and
floodings
have distorted or bent the tree; but changed
it not.
Soldiers from Adrianople, that great city,
from Nikopolis, Arta, Dyrrachium,
rulers from Egripont, dukes from the islands,
youth of the youth of archons.
From Saloniki offshoots, the pallikars strongest,
Saloniki land that is captain and priest,
pallikars strongest
and polemarchs,
from that holy regal city coming,
city in one hand sword, in the other Bible,
on mainland, and on the seas,
the Romaic nation's pride
by its fame and power.
Rivers of Makedon, men of Makedon
met in that City's land are raging,
stand and whip the Bulgar, and down the Slav.

And from all lands nourished by Whiteriver's
  nurses
from Brachoria, Aitoi, the Castle of Angels,
Bonitses, Karpenisia,
the chiefs of Xeromerou, the Baltic pallikars.
They come!
And look! the Zetouniates, Thebans, and some
from all gold Attica, mother of language.
Others younger, more impressive, more pallikar,
but those of Athens still finer
to look on than other men,
with ancient capes, and lofty hats
as though they guarded
in weapons and stance
the traces of former wisdom and fame.
And Liakoura of Livadeia,
Ghiona, Salona's Ghiona,
with flowers of manhood
and Galaxidi;
and pilgrims from it,
its turretbound fort.
And you, you Yanina, Agrapha.
And from the peaks of Roumelia, armatoloi
who making the haunts of wolves and bears
  their haunts
will one day, one day fulfilling fate
—though driven from every place of man—
will preserve the nation's soul, its glory.

No space between. Laborers, peasants follow,
and lead their beasts of labor behind, oxen and
cattle,
their dogs and donkeys and are without number.
People of East and West, festive to circus
or tourney, as though they advance in joy
but forever alert to defend,
straightstance for fighting
and always awaiting the order which bellows:
" Turn lances to ground! Be still! Hold post!
Now keep your distance! Go forward! Strike
home!
Upon them! Now take them! "
And from the ocean they come,
the Sea of Naupactos which Venice has eyed,
from Kypros itself, that famous matrix of
pallikars,
and of songs
forever by Aphrodite praised,
a goddess then, now the Queen
unaging, opposing Digenes,
a star unprophesied that astounds
her island with brilliance.
Battalions of cavalry
from Makedon, Thessaly, Thrace, Epiros;
Byzantine weapons, noted there

for dazzling or shaming,
for admiration, for shame.
Behold! The eaters of Arabs;
the Akrites, mighty palaces'
gatewatch dragons.
Pallikaria
rejoicing at danger day and night
in unwalled clefts
rejoicing in war
masters of Syria, captains by Tigris,
always en route. You know the force of their
hand—
you know, Halepi, Amori,
Konia, Bagdad, Arakleia, Charsiane.
They straddle horses blacker than swallows,
mount horses whiter than doves;
and weave their manes with Venetian jewels;
innumerable golden bells, creating innumerable
echoes.
Their weapons are silver, green their turbans.
Distant in seeing, eagles, like falcons they course,
masters of sword, and first with the lance.
They tread, they shake mountains,
they shout—the pass answers.
With shortlength club the sentry advances to
vigil, hunger,
to slay wild beasts, and skin them there—
he who is sentry; his belt a lionpelt.

He bides his time. A royal marriage is taking
  place
and with his armed hands he rages and snatches
both groom and bride; the marriage is ruined.
And the lowflight partridge he takes
with outspread hand.
Sentries and Akrites advance
and sing of their Digenes, the pride of the king,
and the praise of all manhood,
Romany's maker of peace, destroyer of that
cruel scarecrow Moslem who ruined
oceans, mainlands, all,
plus you, rough Kappadokia,
you, resplendent Smyrna.
And they chant the fight,
of Digenes and Charon on marble floors—
threedays fight and fourdays fight
the death of Digenes
and in Euphrates
his own bier
broad and high, selfbuilt,
and the coming from Tarsos, from Babylon,
of the leaders of Anatolia, commanders of
  legions,
of the guards of the borders, of all the manly,
of all from all regions, to make
the enormous dirge; they came.

The Akrites chant, and say:
" Earth, though you hold him
you devoured him not, you death.
No death for him. He turned to marble. Sleeps.
Will wake? "
Other soldiers chant in their chanting
the mountain birds, the ocean birds of the strada,
which always, as though in answer, endlessly,
quarrel for their fields, and shores, and
mountains.
And others hymn army labors, the conquests of
kings,
in Krete, Dorystolon, Prespa, Zetouni,
and others the sweetness of love's embrace,
the beauty of laurelwed wreathing, the honors
of home,
the cruelness of parting
more black than Hades,
the serpent of mauvaise foi
the cruelty of exile.
And as there races and tongues have met,
so various manners of war meet there.
There are those accustomed to stand
their ground in the open
to hold their thrusts for charging the plain
not to shoot their arrows in flight, or ambush,
and those whose only mastery, in war,

is fighting not on the plain, not
face to face
but always with tricks and guile,
with night and thieving.
And since one warlike king of The City
deep in the shaking of world, its chaos
spread on everyside at barbarians' coming,
since he refound, reseized, rebrought to life
the warlike tactics of worldqueen Rome
and gave it to Romany,
that ruler in Africa, Asia, Europe
she might become;
since that hour, those times, those years
when that great archgeneral, destroyer, creator,
spurred by the blood of Phokad heroes
found on Euphrates waters, in passes of Tauros,
new forms of destruction, new laws of destruction,
creator, founder of klepht and akritic tactics of war
from that time since and from that hour
the soldier of Greece has been arch-technician,
arch-skilled soldier of every encounter, blow, each
weapon, each victory.

In every battalion, every company,
the flames, the flags, the standards upright;
myriad aspect, myriad colored, myriad
brightness.

On some the general commanding, Michael.
Collecting the heavenly ranks, he trumpets
himself,
his glance more sharp than his fiery knife.
Over other ranks eight folds,
eight holy standards, hierarchs who bless and
exorcise.
Over others, marked by crosses, you see Prokopios
the greatsouled hero, Jerusalemite whose sword
the Arabs trembled in Syria.
Over others, the Pantokrator, and the Mother
of God.
Over others, the Theodori, the Great Demetrios,
sire of the Salonikans, all Romany;
yes—and alone—on one shield's center
all alone that beardless chevalier
with Herakles' strength, and Apollo's face.
And behold the flags—
where serpents uncountable whistle
around in their circles,
their heads are fortress,
their mouths are pits,
their bodies whirlwinds.
Prodigies many masked, plumed over with scales.
And on other standards, golden, mother-of-pearl,
a star, a body, weapons, stallion, The City's
Master;
and over them all, a sun of suns, astounding,
awesome,

the labarum,
and around it the chosen fifty.

Daylaborers with leathered flesh
from Makedonian mountains, plains of Thrace,
Kappadokian peasants
Anatolians from Pontos
from that richest garden
of plucked Anatolia
the always savage, separate Karamanites,
scorners of all, scorners even of gods,
wildgame of Lykaonia who grown tame
turn to fearless soldiers;
Armenians of Ararat,
Slavs from Opsiki, from everyplace,
from the land that Sangaros, Maeander enclose
and water.
Soldiers from Pergamon, Miletos, Smyrna;
Amalfians, Venetians, technicians of ocean,
Dalmatians, Chadzaroi. Slavs from Bithynia,
nomads by rivers by lakes
and from the forever watered
fields of Greater Vlachia,
Mirdites from Arvanita, and Arvanites
forever a river whose source
is hidden in darkness, in utter depth.
And the stubborn tribe, which sometimes
cultivates land

and carves it with plow,
and sometimes leaves it, and goes
a life in their tents,
and spreads the trace of its passing
in burnings, and slaughter.
Offspring Paulians, the Mardaites,
marked out with every opprobrium,
the scorn of all who advance unthinking
in herd, and live in blindness and ignorance
teachers and monks and all who preach
or are held in a priestly grasp;
the Mardaites, who worship fire, not gods,
banished and exiled, ikonsmashers,
the Mardaites, Lebanon cedars,
leopards on land, dolphins on ocean,
who raised a bronzen, Taurian castle,
the Mardaites, diking the upheld surging of
  Islam.
These unbent, firmest supports of the Nation,
scattered on every side, to the cities of Thrace,
these from the Lebanese passes, from Armenia,
to Roumely's passes, Morean plains.
And with its captain each tribe passes.
Bardariots, from farthest time
godchildren of Axios,
Romany's heart,
forever surrounded by Slavic tribes,
by raging tribes:
through which one by one they have

changed their faith, but not their language;
they praising the Gospel's God
in tongue that is Turkotartar.
And Persians from the time of Theophilos,
Theophilos their leader once
the only flower of their belief,
whom the Emperor slaughtered,
whom they await till his resurrection,
he who will lead them again as heroes
to victory.
And the unpurged Petsenegoi, corruption eaters,
the pitiless ones. And among the legions
Hungarians too,
scourge of creation, a wrath of God,
a whipping, locusts,
on every side,
poured from vulcan fire,
on every side in the single instant; they burn up
all.
Incomparable horsemen they race
(on horses of wings)
with their unknown bravado, descendants of
Huns.
Among all those who came to The City,
took root, sought a name, and gaining of place,
were the Northern Varangians, " les
Scandinaves."
A hundred only, but worth an army,
nothing obstructs their road.

And Baltic Russians—
the first to come down—
faithful to idols Peroun, maneating Gods,
in lightweight dugouts, the carvedout bodies of
trees.
They startle the Anatolians, Africans,
these Russians
with bodies like palmtrees, like torches, and all
born noble, strong in the hand, like men,
tailbearing men, who show their birth from the
lower world.
Sent from the Tzar to Mother City,
entering the service of The City's King,
they came and stayed; forever profess the Christ,
yet remain idolatrous at the heart.
And there serve also prisoners of war,
and that great slave who ate
the Great King's fifty years
hard, restless years
before he fell genuflect and cut to pieces;
the Istrian Bulgar
the Metsovo Bulgar, with ironchained feet
dragged on; vagrants
and forward the Boyars and Slavs
in dress Byzantines, Skyths in spirit,
a stubborn, highsouled band, heroic,
made of the snake's own poison, and with his
mind;
no matter how you cut

him each cut part
moves and advances forward
having—it seems—each part its proper soul
for living, for living again.
Crowds of unordered people, garrisons.
Into foreign nooks and corners a warlike wind
has cast them, seeded them,
and everywhere, everywhere, they've taken root
till again the hand
of a mighty force has ripped them up
and here then there wars
carnage and storms
drive them on forward, soldiers for fortune.
And the firewinged Katafranks
ever the cavaliers
born from the hippokentaur race
ready ever for charges, reconnaissance,
in fineworked shirts of mail
forever locked, in mail like second bodies,
untouched by sword, untrembling before the
  lance,
cuirassed in brilliance, their blades afire
in the sun, Anatolian sun,
and they enduring that flame
they tireless and moveless, unbowed
by Askalon's sand, or deserts of Gaza.
And Anatolians striking unite their flashing

brocades with the lusterless dyed cloaks
the northern wear, and row after row they pass
polemarchs dressed richly in sable furs
and fighters covered in shirts of beastskin.
And weapons; blunt swords, and longnose lances
on whose small forked flags the angelic
Taxiarch, inscribed, is waving,
Damaskan fabrics, curved two-edged swords.
And weapons for castle demolitions, attacks,
for guarding, for ambush in camps and passes;
and machines for sieging, destroying, in arts
of open war and of klephtic war.
Mail, breastplates of gold, all woven,
carved out, turned, or mastered in form
or cast. And shields from oxhide or iron,
swords, and lances, and scythes, and slings and
  staffs,
with visors, copper helmets, and bows,
and axes and hatchets, and hooks and harpoons,
monstrous machines, spit up—you might say—
from hell itself.
And scattered through ranks the soldier monks
their habits a staining of black on their ridden
  steeds,
their windfoot steeds, their weapons clubs,
and other military monks with bows.
And longlocked priests at head of the line,

golden episcopes, patres in chasubles,
and unstoled hierophants who raise—
for labara—
their longstemmed crosses
filled with holy relics.
And conches and trumpets break forth, go wild,
their tambourines and tympani a thunder,
and hero mouths flow forth, speak forth
and Guiding Mother's hymn is raised to heaven:

" Armyleading Lady, the Spoils to Thee!
The People are weaving your hymn, a woven
  wreath,
with palmleaves numberless, of praise,
numberless adulous lilies,
all for your grace, Who Bore the God!
Lady of Makedon, of The City, of Athens!
Vlacherna swells with your astonishing being.
Destroyer of Skyths, Recourse of the Damned,
Well of Compassion,
Consoler of Being.
Take us from danger of sin. Take pity on us!
Tread to dust
in our midst
the impure vermin of evil reasons.
Your people obey.
Greeting! You bride unwed! "

FIFTH WORD

Genetic land, all in motion of waves within you,
  Greece.
Shore; a trembling in your still surface falls.
A woman's body; and all you are—from peak to
  hollows
aerily, proudly, is blending, immobile.

All-drinking time has crossed your face:
as though you changed your faith and changed
  your name,
named now Megalovlachia, and under the tread
of the Goth, the Hun, the Serb, the Vlach
are convulsed as you were convulsed before
under other tread with other names; yet
  Thessaly
always you are.
Godforms and gods first
fountained to life in you.
Now greetings!
Your earth is polycarp, river-nursed,
your fields are dew and rich, your passes broad,
your grassy richness flowers, whiffs like honey
for your herds to graze in,
to increase and harvest.

Like your polycarp earth
Imagination in you
bore fruit
sweetfused with Hellenic thought
and mothered Greekchild vision, myths,
the poets' joining, idols of the elite,
and ageless now as then,
still joys to the world,
and against them nothing to match,
an only match those marvelous Tempes
they too mythic in kind, and virgins of nature.
Laborous horses are yours, but your sons are
soft,
as if witched by nereids, are men under spells,
yet more than your horses, worse than your sons,
your women are ragers, dreads of the night,
go maddening by magic like hags, those fruits
of your soil
they measure the treeleaves, number the stars,
in their passing whip and milk the moon
and pull it down, and play with pearls in their
hands
and gather locoweed, pick devilgrass
and potable mayweeds, offering; drinks
filled with love and loathing, with
final adieux
to your wits.
Your fame is greater in Myth's caress

than in History's voice; your fame
announces your nobleness, your ancient fame,
firstwritten in the golden book of the Greeks
in the ancient time when Kentaur, immortal
  Kentaur,
fountain of every knowledge, of every art,
a pride of the gods,
nourished with foam, with the milk of birds,
with the lion's marrow, the orphic lyre—
nourished that dream of the manly, that hero,
Homer, who swells,
your *Iliad*, song of songs.

And nowhere has the land such bounty,
ever poured in evenness, boldly as possible,
(as though creation were always formed
with the mind of art)
no nowhere has land such bounty
like the airhung bounty of
cliffs, your cliffs, your cliffs
the upstraight introduction into your land:
cyclop mainland cliffs, and scyllan ocean cliffs,
approachless, isolate, incomparable, smitten
upward by cataclysm, before world itself and
  its light;
cliffs like pits, to hold above them
highraised altars of what godbeings?

idols of what deniers of world?
who knows?
Cliffs where only the clouds of heaven
taking original faces
taking a thousand amazing, undrawn faces,
in their wilderness, beauty, pass
in comparable beauty.
And now, behold, especially for this they have
grown
to receive and guide
to greet with greeting
the path of the victorious adulant people.
Foliaged Pelion, a lofty sentry
addressed them; its succulent oaktrees
murmured the news
and its savage chestnuts; Kissavos saw them
made signs to Olympos which raises its vision
like something more high, still more apart,
Olympos ever the haunt of armatoloi and gods
and a word that those mountains whispered
the neighborers heard it,
Salambrias heard it—
who courses among them royally, pomp,
a lord of the mountains, the fields,
and holds them apart, the leventi-twin
mountains,
and keeps them lest they, the forever hostile,
fight;

he heard it, spread it through tributaries
digested within himself, creating from them
his distant and broad extent, his giant thrust.
And look, Pharsalos its river!
And the ancient Apidanos!
Its name forgotten
and yet it holds, in its memory bound
it holds and mutters of wars
passions of polemarchs
(who passed) and shaped their words,
of polemarchs who paused for breath at river's
edge,
men worn by shame
or borne on the wings of conquest.
Flowings, sidestreams, rivers
from the hour when they first knew life
in the ridges of Metsovo
from then to their loss of self
in White Sea depths
remembering they had not seen
remembering never was seen, so
broadly, on every side, so flooding,
like some huge overflowing, a flooding of
weapons,
an overflowing of pallikars,
through Thessaly all
through Hellenic heartland
and on to Athens.

The hour had not rung in
the inlaid lyre not come
lyre carved from druid wood
with golden strings,
in the candid Olympic light
with Harmony's hands to string the magician's
   passing
the passing wandering German
who seemed to spring from the Rhine its nereids
in the midst of shieldstrong Varangian riders
a leader destructive, creative,
hastening to Sparta,
groom in search of that bride of thought, white
   Helen,
such as she'd come to him in magic mirror,
as angels gaze toward the Virgin's throne,
two worlds that melt to a newborn world.
And for his escort Manto the prophetess,
Sirens, nereids, lamias, kentaurs,
ancient these daimons and modern.
Enchanted Peneios flows, dreaming
it runs in brilliance
down amaranthine Elysian fields.
But for me the hour has rung. A haunted flute,
of what I am quite unworthy I chant,
of another passing, another race, another greatness.

By the mountain of Gkoura they passed
the Zetounian gulf laughed out
its azure laughter on them.
And the outstretched plain you cross, Alamana,
received them, and to the myrtles
the rushes spoke,
the shrubs to the trees, the trees to the birds;
cranes and doves, the birds of prey
from the larks of dawn to the evening locusts
from eagle to butterfly
all—whatever has wing or voice,
will live for months and years
in thought of this dreamlike passing.
                                        They went and trod
The Pass, enlarged by the bodies
of the Spartan king, and of the Three Hundred,
made by them a world.
And Kallidromo they saw
and over Hypate the Pit, her
sentry; before them, opening out,
phantasm, Alamana, which
castle was built,
from bones of men and of horses,
upraised by the soldiers of Heavenly Nikephoros:
river's dowry of bones.
Fortress, allwhite gleaming fortress in sun

chanting the Hellenes who slaughtered the
Bulgar.
Fortress, allwhite forever glistening fortress
under moon, in all of its brightness.
With another whiteness.
The merest touch of a dreamfilled ray
wakened within it the soul of ghosts
and something turned it to spirit of night
to trap and to something shrouded
tightened in shroud with millions of folds.
Spirit of night, at its feet went winding the
Alamana,
its stream, and see how it waters those walls
that they may thirst less
that they find some pausing
till it drop in sleep its unkinged eyes.
For the fortress, mighty fortress of bones,
thirsted a hard, a total thirst,
forever it stayed apart, a phantom cursed,
the giant skullmade fort
which water could never quench
which longed for nothing like water
which longed for blood.
It thirsted for blood, it longed for
blood poured into the depths of Alamana,
to draw in the river's extra blood
to spread it through its own veins,
to enter creation and life again.

And the King of Constantinople,
King the Cliff,
when he saw with his eyes those haunted walls
could not prevent a shudder's
passing through his still heart, a mereness of
   shudder,
that man who'd known no shudder
then (his hour most brutal and worthless)
when before him passed—at his own command—
the manly warriors of battered Samuel,
doomed to eternal hell of blindness,
led—each regiment—by a crippled one-eye,
and before their unspeakable faces, victim of fate,
the blasted tzar fell prone
      as from hatchet of lightning.

On to Salona they went, and all the cataracts
down the surrounding mountains greeted with
   thunder.
The florid gardens, yes in all that growing
behold the Salonan olive, thicker, fuller.
Attica's holy olive
is the very shape of idea, ideal,
but the olive here is longed-for, firmed-out flesh.
The mountains are darkness among the firs,
or among the clouds. Passes and meadows
gardened by water and wealthy with trees,

and spreading particular shadows like reasonings,
firs and oaks, and pines and planetrees,
some of them strict on the mountain sides
or straight on the peaks,
and others bent to the rivers, ever inbound to
the rivers.
From the midst of Kallidromo, from the heart
of Oeta
down from Parnassos, the streams come flowing,
and wind like snakes and pour in playings like toys
into the plain to meet
Kephisos that draws them in through an instant,
and they seem to stop with a sudden halt
as though to match their stride with the army's
stride.
Gulfs and rivers, passes and bays, ridges and
clefts,
mountains standing apart forever
mountains conjoined, mountains illustrious,
mountains extinguished from memory
though inextinguishable parts of creation
mountains by any name—
Vardousia, Gkiona, Oxia, Chlome, The
Prophet Elias, Velouchi,
and Dove, the summit of two-backed Pindos,
and ridge that rejoiced in your enemy's slaughter
by Greeksharp swords: and call yourself
from that time The Bulgar Mountain!

With the fragrant breath of your pines
with your lustrous upslope firs,
and your higher heights, from your naked slopes
  and snows
you saw them pass; and see them still, in your
  dreams,
which reach forth farther than eagles' seeing!

They had seen Parnassos; a boy, a soldier
thought of his mother,
and like a psalm, an echo—
plain and mysterious—
and smelling of incense:
" On the slope of Liakoura a church is built
a locked-up church.
And whoever passes hears the voices.
As of men who chant, make liturgy:
and whenever the water floods flood down
and root up all
if you come toward the closed-off church
there is shift of course
the flood detours
to leave you in peace."

And Parnassos has heard the passing, and
  watches the people,

and opens itself a song—for it is entirely song,
a song to remain unsilenced,
a song from root to peak, like the Flute myself.
And mouths and lyres sang out that song
the mouths of
all that bloom and fly and stir and stay
on the mountain's slopes and passes
and caves and peaks:
" Double my peaks have been, double my name,
Old Man Parnassos I, and Liakoura the young.
A rocky androgyne, a two-in-one,
a tightbound, unloosed union,
a world, a creation:
and however unreconciled these seem to be,
I join these two unjoinables.
I am man the cosmos and woman, a creation,
an ancient cosmos,
new sun ever, among the stars
of the intelligible sky.
The two all holy forces, light and water, here
took flesh, took shape, were makers:
the one arose as god, was called Apollo,
the other grew to goddess, became the goddess,
Muse ninefold, and Muse ninesouled
and nine times mother.
And the lightborn one with the dewpoured one
wove loves, danced dances here
danced godful dances.

Just look!
Around my feet the airlight temple
with the wax of bees, the down of the swan,
the heart of the world, the praise of the world
of men;
the blood of the serpent laid its base,
and stones of lightning fell from the stars
and the dolphins wove
patterns along the coast,
laboring for the temple's fame.
And the Delphic prophetess, her holy ravings,
melt in the sound of my mountain murmur,
Castalia gives water to Pegasos
and raises him, and balsams all.
And in the face of the cosmos I, who
without a death yet lost myself
to shine on the heights of Thought,
I a creation from fire, from dew, from flesh,
and hands and eyes and ears I fill
with body, line, and sound
each time they hear me, touch me, see me.
And I am as though outpoured
a woman at her fruiting time
and though ready to bear in ripeness
I stand in my beauty still.
Now gods and goddesses exist no more
no more the paeans and priests, the prophetess,
miracles,

the idols, oracles, and temples,
the treasuries, the youth;
all go.
The ikons are buried, rubbled,
rubbed into dust by barbaroi,
driven away by the Galileans
and turned to daimons, to ghosts of the other
  world;
until the time shall come that they will resee the
  sun
in the workshops of scholars, the tombs of beauty,
and remains and rubble will be worshiped again
more longingly, fully than anything whole.
The life of the living has ruined you, forever;
but I have not died with you, I exist forever!
  See me!
With all that is passing, with all that lasts
and with all of the dreams you were
with all of the things you are;
the mists and the rocks live here, a life as
  brothers.
All here are mists and dreams.
For the God who is god over gods
and has no name
is hastening to ruin them—the great, the small—
all things he has made,
whatever is beautiful,
whatever the soul bends down to praise.

And powerfully, forcefully,
with that same zeal he raises
the destroyer's hand above them all,
and whatever he sees that quake
has battered, he disassembles.
Not that creation is pitiless, indifferent;
the Creator is hidden, wordless, and unexplained;
He drives on all, and longs to accomplish,
a god above gods, to accomplish
incomparable works.
And whatever is ancient
(or toppling)
he puts aside
to run his mystic way unblocked,
he strikes for a world more full
and more complete than this.

I am two-peaked creation and show myself
from far in all-white turban, geranium cloaks;
sometimes my sides and clefts are red
and naked, sometimes wear blouses of fog,
a cloth of mist:
like rainbows I contain all colors
joining them, sporting them as I wish.
And my cliffs are fortresses,
my firs an army,
the birds my people, the eagles my generals.

And on my highest peak, untouched Lykeri,
a crystal palace of sun is burning
where the Northwind sits, is fortified
a tyrant among the elements, a dragon of winds,
the first of my pallikars, ambassador.
My springs are rich, my winds caressing
and as deep as my caves, that broad are my wells
for the innocent flocks: the shepherds lead them there
to the wellnursed grazing grounds, to slake their thirst.
And I have scorned nothing;
the sheep-pen arouses my pride
as a temple would,
and I hear the cuckoo's voice with the same
religious awe I hear above me
the clouds contestant and loud with lightning.
The milk from my goats I pour as gift,
a white liqueur,
and my broad fruit-bearing plains are swollen
with famous fruit, and bright-orange wheat.
I have my despairs, my bitterness,
my thoughts, my passions that burn and weaken,
my nights with no following sun,
my reasonings that turn and twist
insoluble enigmas

that show, enclose more bitter a thousand times
that give returned more bitterly
what blacknesses and cruelties
the world itself reveals.
Within me is heard the dirge of the world
poured forth more acrid,
as by chants of a multitude.
And if you do not believe it, advance and hunt
through some of my caverns, my caves,
which never have seen the sun,
ever on guard, and closing, within them,
specters, specters who weep,
enslaved, who loving the sun
yet seek it in vain,
and weep their tears
which turn to stone.
And alone the echo suffering, paeans
at times and questions the specters, and they
reply to him groaning, with gasping weepings,
and whip their breasts
in number a hundred specters, even a thousand.
And if some mortal makes his way to those
 depths
led along by a torch's brilliance
under the shining of his torch a greater
darkness is drawn, a thicker darkness
outfolded.
He sees.

And now in my houses, and under my roof—
as though it were all my family—I love
that man the most who is lowly of family
or repute, a shepherd with flocks.
A hymner with flute,
one who worships the past, or a certain hermit
or antartes with club of iron.
The simple and humble I love,
and the men, exiled from the world,
who come to climb, untired by my ascent,
unfrightened by my rough visage.
To the Freer they come to catch their breath,
to keep their honor, for staying free,
for relighting the fire, for drawing in new
lifestrength from my clean air, clean water.
For down on the land are the evil and lazy
the fields are for slaves.
But these I gather, care for, and guard:
the hand that resists, the mouth
that fountains with song. Enough:
I remember my stones, one time.
They rolled from the heavy treadings . . .
my bushes screeled, the wild birds screamed;
I see the leventis, bodies like willows, they climb
my cliffs and my slopes.

'Who are you ?' 'God only knows who we are,
just
call us: orphans of Hellenism, bastards of Fate.'
'Where from?' 'Olympos.' 'Have gods
invited you, called you to festivals,
to pour you the godly wine up there
in the brilliant air where bodies are light?'
'Your language is odd, eludes my mind.
On Olympos are nesting birds, wild wolves
dwell,
the passes unnumbered, the snows untouched,
the haunts untaken, and the pallikars
men, decided and weaponed.
They place their dwellings there
and their forts of stone
and they raise the free man's life
for resurrection, strange new homeland.
And now we've divided up;
wherever mountain, a haunt.
We came to you, ancestor, that our fire
might blaze in the thunder of war.
We too creators—with weapons—of Idea.'
Be welcome, pallikars!
I stay Parnassos, though now Liakoura,
and I am ever that temple which god
has never abandoned
God by whatever name.

And you who pass so grandly from here
before whose treading the earth is shaken,
trembles;
immeasurable, sudden people, led
by a pitiless Hero, a king, cavalier
apart, worth you all—
the sweat of a thousand journeys drops from
your bodies,
in your eyes burn fires of a thousand wars;
it is as though you went—not as before
to ruins and bleeding, suddenly, fatally—
but somewhere else, joyful, and festal,
to religious worship, the festal;
advance, and hear me, people, and break your
course
come here and bend, bend genuflect,
bend worthy before your god, whatever god,
from my twin peaks.
And your oblation will be received, your prayer
raised high,
by holy unmade lovely images,
rayed through by sunrays' sleepless
golden candle,
all images that stand widesowed, seen ordered
from here, Salona, to the sea down there
Salonika's Sea,

to the Holy Mountain;
Romaic capes and mountains, and all the shores
that play forever erotic, and melt in vaginal bays
yes all that are columned erect and all that
   recline to take
the blues the greens the reds of blood
from my blood brother Helikon
to the vigil of skytall distant Taygetos."

SIXTH WORD

Emerged on the broadlaid plain of Livadeia,
in Livadeia, that polity set over
the entrance of a sharpcrest valley;
Erkuna waters that valley
Erkuna infant of Helikon,
small drywater, growing growing
as though it drank in every snowfall
with water of that Icyspring that
sped it forward first
and with other waters borne
from thousands of water pipings
from hearts of crags.
Clear springs, fountains, highfounts, spouts,
mysterious you are, are hamadryads
with uncaught dewformed bodies,
naked beauties, and with you
shameless satyrs—the voices of men
the rutting of beast, their signs—made love.
Clear springs, fountains, plashing spouts,
and foams, and splashings of dew, and waves
and snakes of water
less than the bodily longing of women,
demonic and magic, goddesses, weirdesses, always, however, lovely, always in grace,
always the givers of freshness, and always borne
back,

as in the beginning,
to the arms of Creation;
appearing, without a change, the same as yourselves,
at the passing of foreigner men and heroes
and ready at every time—
even to them—to offer yourselves
as though they were Tritons and Satyrs and Pans.
Mount of Livadeia, behold Laphysti! New
despots have not yet crossed it,
providing it other fates
and leaving their footprints in the stones,
and ardent Bakkhos, the mystic Bakkhos
has escaped that valley completely
of his holy traces leaving
not the slightest print.
Goes forth the Urold mantic babbling,
Trophonios, that lasttongue bird
in the silence of all the others,
and all of the swamplands opened
and only the sacred height, the height of
Orchomenos,
cyclopic remnant
and here, and there, on everyside,
remains and rubble
that once were camps and temples, citadels,
cities,
and are no more, and endure in falseness,
and do not remain,

as Nature remains, addressing them always all.
And crowds crowd forward to greet, a various
  crowd,
come men of the fields, of camps, come masters,
  hired hands,
indigenous, outland, mixed,
who work on the sea, on land,
all the withered shoots of the ancient trunk
and other green branches raised
to life by barbarous new grafting
a world of slaves, whether laborer, idler,
a multiple world
is there as sudden as buildings raised
somehow in violence, suddenly: huts and houses
  and towers,
villages, camps, and churches and sketes and
  walls of forts,
with force and constraint raised up,
from one night to the next,
and raised over ruin and rubble,
rubble known once as temples and castles and
  palaces
with gold on their summits, iron at their roots,
and marble and marble.
And from those remains
and over those ruins, with those same stones,
on the same foundations, the new shapes rise
till some new cataclysm seizes,

some new maker shapes them
to the order of some new rhythm.
And the laborer, leaving the plain,
vintners, their vineyards,
shepherds, men of affairs, artisans, hurry
holding forth ikons, cherubim, lamps,
scatter branches along the roads,
spread garments along the roads,
that the king may pass; knees bent to him.
And the savior passes, the enslaver passes,
and hears the hymnings of praise, but the
  hymners
are empty of heart, of conviction,
and the free man's wings beat not in their joy,
the free man's soul, his spark.
On the public road that runs toward Thebes
the gardens are waiting
thickleaved for nightingales again
on the outspread wings of an April
and waiting they see the black
black lightninged cloud, and long in secret.
From the well-built monasteries emerge
the wearers of habits, emerge and praise; the
  church-
bells strike the monk in the skete's heart.
And only the ruins remain unstirred, the towers
of ancient Hellas. To holy Eleusis
Kephisos no longer runs, as always,

its usual course from the foot of Kithairon;
now its route is swifter, it runs
to empty its news at once
in Athena's ears.

See twopeaked Helikon that flows from Thebes
to the ruins of Korinth, then down to the
Isthmos.
Here Helikon, there the Sphinx' own mountain,
neighbor mountain; the Muse's castle
the ruin for the ruinous hag who uttered
the unlockable prophecy; like neighbors they
stand,
the deeplaid puzzle of cosmic mind
and the song of the heart, the simple and lovely
song,
the song of the heart in creation.
And Gypsycastle too, a ruin, on mountain rubble
on Kithairon's narrows; Akritic water,
that inwalled watches the boundaries of Athens.
On Kithairon's peak flows an icecold stream
and the vigiling Akritas falls prone, and adulates,
and the icecold fountain Kithairon makes
mouthful of brilliance, utterance:
" Now the Firred they have named me,
my summits lofty—as ever, so now.
So, greetings, my pallikars!

And to You My King!
May you pass over
me, contemplate heaven and stars,
and take pride in the earth
with its lawn of bright flowers."
And what shall I put first, what narrate
first by song, and what shall I
put first of what they see and tread
and feel, encounter,
like dreams of dawn, like ghosts of night—
O Earth—which ever you labor
strongly, fruitfully, equally Eros and Death,
under the sun that founds new temples
with ruins of the old,
rejuvenates all.

And they saw Thebes, Boeotia's heart, upon
its Ancient Fort: a magic music raised
it—Lyre, more powerful than Kyklops' hands.
There near Ismenos river they saw Thebes
the city heaped with pitiless evils,
heaped and piled,
and each more vicious than the last;
the reckless polemarchs
" good " Alexander, Sulla,
Huns and Romans, Goths, Makedonians,
and more,

Alaric's cavalry, the tread of Samuel.
Yes, they saw Thebes the famous
whose purple dyes are no longer dyed
with the flowing blood of wars,
whose dyes are worked by
craftsmen into simple silks.
But Thebes has forgotten its splendid swan—
great among the great—
and peaceful, turns in peace,
conforms its original unformed lays
to the loom and its rhyme;
a worker with hands of gold.
Yes, they saw Thebes. Had eyes myopic
whose shadows the Emperor's brilliance
  scattered,
had ears like heavy weights, those Barbaroi,
listenwide only to trumpet blasts,
to the savage orders of polemarchs,
extruded in various tongues,
extruded to right and left;
and did not hear, and did not see
the giant vision of the Askraian,
singer who passes in evening dirging
forth beside Dirke waters and mixes
his bitter tears into murmuring springs
and stirs them, troubles them,
and weeps for his ruined Thebes;
for that one chosen, that only son of song

has won the grace
to know in present, future, and past,
and weeps for the dreads of life, the fall of man,
the falseness of woman, slavery's sting
and later the bitter indifference of Nature,
Lamia, compound of famine,
plaguing, hailstones;
he weeps for weakness, enslavings, bad luck,
annihilation; the thousand evils
here, in all of Greece—
evils which fall like snow on Helmos,
flake on flake, and here today
and there tomorrow different
races, tribes, endure them.
He weeps for the bitterest slavery
the mighty destruction fated
sooner or later
from Asia's depths.
Behold, behold!
This hour it starts, it fights to spread
like a night that hell has freed
and first appears, on Armenian borders,
the Persian's heir,
later heir of the Saraken,
and first appears, behold,
that curse the Turk!

The springs are many-fountained, the geysirs
endless, unsilenced in their plash.
And they water the berry-shrubs
pass among the willows
and play in swiftness with those willowtresses
until they reach the breast of Dirke, and are
poured,
pour troubling it, creative springs, creative
geysirs.
Dirke, hail! If you have changed your noble
name,
are called Plakiotissa, then I, the foreign flute,
shall call you such, call you that bluntly,
and ornament your newfound name
with all my rhythm's power, with all music,
and slowly form your name
for the coming challenges
that will come, will find you,
you and we who have, in you, a single home.
Thus the naked, unadorned walls of a simple
hut—
walls white or blackened with smoke—
are adorned with flowers by a caring hand
for joining of newlyweds, who spend their night.
And Dirke, you, and with you all
that springs and flows like you,
the rivers, fountains, springs,
and wells and streams

and drystreams, greenlands, fields, and
mountains, forts,
from Olympos snows to the star of Athens,
every portion, mother Greece, of your
pure body,
you very you, as loudly as I am able, Greece,
with your new name I call you,
whatever be fated that you shall suffer,
be scorned, and die in this newer name
(forever like gods; however
the weight of their loss and death
sooner or later they tread
down death and return to light)
with your new name I shall call you,
Romaiosyne!
With your new name I crown,
and seeing how fully this crown
befits your head, myrtle-girded head,
or akanthos-girded;
I tremble and cry with joy.
And with your new names I address
I who am echoer of fate, and history's herald
who bring the extinguished to light again
that it may grant again its flame
the spark now buried deep in ashes
becoming flame; that it may bake our bread,
or light our fires
I breathe audacity, arouse the world,

the world scorned by the petty
by the myopic.
If wise men leave you from their records
if men ignore you
still nightingales chant on.
I snatch you from their chantings,
the names that you have worn and names
not yet put on,
will wear tomorrow;
to all of you all hail
now and tomorrow
hail to you all
places ancient, though baptized a modern name.
So the newwed bride
without a tear exchanges
ancient gloried name for new
unknown, which her own lover owns (whoever
he).
Her longing makes lover's new name,
like lover himself, desired; it makes her proud
in whatever walk—success or failure—
in whatever fate
to carry that name.

SEVENTH WORD

Morning, a day sunpoured and beautiful with sun
and Athens sapphire stone of earth's own ring.
Light on everyside, forever light,
and light shows all—in roundness, stalactitic,
behold—it leaves no thing mysterious
unanalyzed, uncertain
if it is dream
mere foam, or firmness.
Mighty and humble objects appear the same.
Pentele's peak, or tiny asphodel;
the brightbrowed temple, the pale anemone;
all weigh the same
in Creation's scale.
Light, these you bring to us, bring near,
these light brings out,
each unique.
The gulf of Aigina shines whitely, poured
by brilliance; light nears it to
the highwaved etchèd hillsides;
and the deep highheaven, marked
by only the black of a bird, the white of a cloud,
light nears to the shore of mountains,
it nears to the slopes of mountains
nears the mountain's peak to the
olive trees of the plain

and the field, light nears to the coast
and the boats of the coast advance
to their homelike sheds beside
the land, calmly to beach themselves.
And all, all shown, by light,
borne in the air to nearness, as though light
might fuse them in passion to single dance
that each might meet in the other's embrace.
So on every side the mountains,
wooded Parnes, ivory Hymettos, light
Pentele stand, are seen,
lie one (in that air) with the lighter etched
more distant met
high mountains of Hydra, of Nauplia,
of Damalas, Korinth:
the hills and crests and clefts and cliffs and
  coasts,
Tripyrgi, Phaleron, Piraeos, ports and harbors,
immortal Salamis, austere Psyttaleia
to where that royal crown has topped
a temple shown from every side,
tops highland Sunion.
And the Attic ocean coast—
cut to apartness from White Sea—
lives on in its mother's arms,
nobler and bluer than she.
Today firstseen, something astounding, see,
its marks beyond the field, beyond

the thickness of olive groves it spreads
intent and wholly intent toward that magic mesa,
still small (in sight) yet higher than Olympos.
There an unshaken life, a haunted land,
immortals and mortals of marble, the stone
a flower from beauty, star flower from mind
and a simple spirit, to support
the enormous weights.
That temple of music—on mesa enchanted—
is raised for a crown over all around
over goods of the land
over beauties of Being,
itself yet fairer and better made.
Forever the fountains of myth flow there,
historical springs, and their springing
and flow is forever
the springing of joy and of praise,
of Athena; forever.
And always the Doric temple, simple,
great to the triple degree,
its thinnest line drawn true,
rooted in iron and winged it meets,
is pliably whole, unbendably whole.
Creation that filling your eyes
rejoices your eyes,
and stands like something intelligible,
and every line of it
and every rounding incomparable

reflecting, speaking.
And ever its brows and flanks
and ever its columns, friezes, summits,
with their sacred carvings, their shining
runes, and eagles, astragaloi,
the waves and serpents and roses,
from green of tree to the yellow of ochre,
the carvings, images, statues,
those that from walls of red
stand forth, alive, stand woven together
woven as they are,
the heroic figures of Athens, the precious objects
of State,
the carvings so lightly carved
they open to eye's mere touch—
from blue profound—
religious forms, of a worship
entirely joy, of a life entirely flower.
And always twelve gods for regents
of the cosmos that stands unrulable
having found an immaculate life
in the heaven of Art.
And all is born from Athena,
yet her birthcoming is not
the coming to birth of a child;
is ripe, is clear in her panoply,
her glance has measured the other gods in an
instant

for startled, astonished they are by her sudden
  striking,
so sudden she strikes, so wholly she flies.
And always the Amazons, one
breasted Lamias, run,
unbound on unbound horses
and ever stronger leventes of Athens
cut down that course by Ilissos water.
And the wavestruck lord of the sea
contests with the queen of Wisdom,
and Athena is kingdom, is victor,
for Mind is stronger than waves of the sea.
And ever in a giant struggle of forms,
of horses and men intwined,
against heroes who have from nature
no strength but what is human,
flesh, and in it heart,
a struggle of Kentaurs who batter Lapiths
of Lapiths who force the Kentaur to kneel.
And ever the maidens who bear in their hands
shovels the priestess has blessed
and for their baskets
swollen with branches and fruits of Demeter
supports are the finecarved heads of maidens.
And handed from priest to pallikar's hands
the sumptuous, thousand embroidered
Athenian peplos passes, waving.
And ever, to the end of vision, the waved sea stirs

the double advance to the goddess, here
to Lepsina's Lady, there
to the goddess of Athens.
The procession is ready, yet has not started,
the sweet uneasy instant of thought
the hour the living hour when you
strain, you tend, you probe, you feel
and are felt, are delighted—
no second time will be yours for such joy—
for you have been touched by bliss
(in the hour of waiting,
always finer than the hour of having).
And ever, from one day to the next,
the groups—here more thin, there denser—
gather, are woven, advance in rhythm;
and some, from the sunset point, advance to
 the north,
and others go east, from the north.
These are aristocrats, and le peuple,
are virgins, crowned cattle for sacrifice,
and slowdrawn wagons,
are supple bearers of baskets,
are runners, passing the torch
and last, swift horsemen who follow
with all the graces of their youth,
their irreproachable graces,
of flesh, of stance, of dress and nakedness,
who make the festival of man the joy of god.

And so the Immortals
forever unwatched observe the procession
in the midst of the people they love
the Immortals rejoice
in the midst of the mortals, the barely different;
Immortals apart these are,
Demeter, Asklepios, Kastor and Pollux,
and clubbearing Herakles, huge,
and Kore the ancient,
goddess broadthroned with her mighty staff.

Today first seen, something astounding, see,
breaks forth, and a trembling awakens entirely
among the godlike immortal figures,
amazement wakes, a second conversion to marble
a second, more powerful forming
that holds, that restrains
the greatjoyed idols, and later drives them to
trembling
striking with lightningstroke swiftness
a swiftness more swift than the course of a
thought
cast through time and space.
The choruses startled, astounding
in circles of mortals surpassing the mortal
of gods created with the very essence
of the bodies and souls of men.

The groups and those who are lone
and the battles and sacrifice
and the silent speeches, the unvoiced songs,
whatever the infantry, the chevaliers
imagine, express, what they fight for and bear,
and those who are bent or straight
or seated—the goldmouthed philosophers, all
thought—
and the demigods in their calm and the heroes
of war
the young men, the women, the children, old
men, and infants,
the nobles, the lines of the poor,
the nobles in silk, the others
more richly yet in naked flesh;
and all, who were carved about and
grew below and above, on every side
of the heights and depths of the cliffdeep temple
which they make planet;
that entire enchanted land is seized
to be changed today, and you see—they begin
to enter the other life that holds
us within itself;
from longing this life rolls forth,
from caring it lives.
As though, grown into manness
from worlds of myth,
some exorcist had drawn to life
and touching this world awoke it

and raised it slowly from sleep,
and as yet you cannot quite assert
its awaking,
nor say " it is still asleep,"
to this marbled thing.
My god! Halfwakened, and this halfwakening
arouses old certain pains
black and wretched evils
which torment this our land
its gods and men.
For though gods are higher than mortals
(as the Muse the Tragic Muse remarked,
that queen among Muses,
and you dripped, O bitter word,
through the country of sweetness),
we know that above the gods, above them all,
a power rides, rides over divinity: A Fate.
Yet, for the knowing such shakings, astonish-
ments,
halfwakings, the weight
of the flesh of a man
is too much.
Only if somewhere here pass by
us souls released from their bodies
breaths passing by
if angels fly past—then only you,
O angels, O souls, and you—
daimones of ocean, and spirits of land,
and geists of the world

and all of the limber shadowy beings
the relics of all the religions
new worship's ascetic matterless relics
and you the ancient and exiled gods
(now turned into nightmares and demons
and flying through night from the altars,
the pitiful relics, and
forever across the land
of their growth and greatness . . .
assuming other faces, other names,
and beneath them all invisible, unmovable,
demanding from old believers the old beliefs,
with only another name;
the gods in exile saying:
" Christians you call yourselves, yet are always
  idolaters!"):
then only, you, spirits of this and another
  kosmos,
can know and behold before you
the startling unsettling of spirit world.
Thus the eye sometimes, the ear sometimes
can grasp in its silence and slightness
a stirring on waters, a breath in the hillside
as proof that a hand has grasped its creation.

Today in all perfect and chiseled things
in achievements of art or scenes of creation

which you know at once, can grasp at once,
can suppose you might stretch your hand
to them, can suppose you might find them all
in hand for touching, for palping—
out there, half-starting, astounding, to form for
  the eye,
emerging from slopes of Kithairon,
by Eleusis in the stretch of the road that led
mystic litanies to the City of Wisdom—
see something of dust, behold! Like duststorm,
it all drives forward and rises and grows
  entirely
and in the brilliance of light it shows more
  darkly
and at one time it is a cluster of clouds, then a
  forest,
sometimes it lightnings, its thunder you wait
to thunder, and then it will be
the glass of a lake, it nears
and it is the tread of an army,
the brilliance of weapons.

And the farseeing Mesa, the Mesa stirred
inquires and considers, and opens
its myriad mouths and speaks
and its speaking the first sound life
at the crack of day:

" Ruler of Rome, apostle of the Word,
final spokesman of the Sun, the first among the
first,
does not a general a victor, the Stander Beside,
attain to my broken altars, to raise them again,
does not a saving one bring back—
a freer of them from east and west—
bring back my long gone marble, entrails,
from the prisons of pirates, the hands of thieves?
Barbarian among his kind,
with every scorn for the life of stone,
for all immortal thoughts of mind,
returns King Alaric? Is it not
that from Attic villages where sturdy
olive forever shadows—
your shading is always the olive—despite the
sun—
is it not that Dexippos again,
the final child of this land,
saver, uprighter of a downbent world
comes to baffle the Goth and Herulian in
ambush
Dexippos forever of Athens, in love
with sword and idea
who appeared like a freshwater spring
in a region scorched after earthquake fire? "

And the farseeing Mesa, haunted Mesa
groans and ponders, and opens
all of its thousand, myriad mouths,
and speaks, and its speaking
a mother's at the bier of her only child:

" My god! the burning is vast, the water mere
 drop,
and deliverance a flash of lightning, and
dream the undersupport.
Are you the land where bees nursed with honey
from the flowered lips of your Holy Sage?
On you two lamps for your road and greatness,
gold lamps, shone, unmade by hands,
O land, and your holy Wise Man has lighted
the one for you, has raised it as peak
on a mighty column
that his light be unclouded, that you be its sky.
The other the weaponed goddess, your guardian
 virgin,
has hung for you in her splendid temple,
a timeless light, for you; for you it shone.
And the first lamp lighted the bending
of your mind toward contemplation, its depths,
toward knowing's immenseness
where stands, and plumbs the kosmos,
reflective Wisdom.

And the other lamp rayed out
over the rising of your heart
toward Wisdom Effectual, the manna
of manliness, the ocean—unstill—of war.
Two lamps, and the brighter you could not
 determine,
two stars, from their double light
your existence depended.
And the first lamp has gone out
and the other goes . . .
and the mighty column stands
like a headless mast,
and now a third lamp takes its place
the lamp of another faith, of the lawless foreign
Hebrew Lady.
The holy Wise One dies, heirless departs,
and from her lovely temple your virgin
 guardian
has gone, your goddess, lost, not to return.
And all has denied you, you the denier of all,
and all has been driven from you, alas!
the last of the lovers of wisdom, those seven
your very womb
now weakened shoots; one day, behold!
they are fled to the King of Persia
in the change of times,
(You Earth, who slaughtered Xerxes, gave
 Aischylos life)

the final philosophers, those seven, your very
womb,
those sons of the Persian-destroying world
gone to the Persians
those sons gone begging a corner of land
to build a temple
for no more place do they find in Greece
for making their temple, establishing
in it again the dismounted image
they took with them, hailed as Wisdom,
believing that it was Greece
the ageless Greece
this pitiful saved wood form."
And the farseeing Mesa, stirred Mesa
inquires and considers, and opens
its myriad mouths and speaks
and its speaking like tripled
hail that whips the landscape:

" Do not they return, as they then returned
pursued by the shade of the Persian king,
strangers within their exile
strangers in their own country
the group's last palpitation of life
the last of these lovers of wisdom
do not they return to close
their eyelids at my cliff's foot,

for before them I hold my plateau locked,
I bereft of Athena, now slave of The Other?
Or is this the Lady returned who was lost
of whom none know—did she die,
relive, find some monument fitting
or other heavens—does that Lady, great Lady,
return to her former throne on the Walls,
does she wield her spear, control that servant—
forever behind her, the servant Nike—
in her winged car that breathes, itself a soul,
does she carry chryselephantine arms,
is her flesh of bronze, is her height of mind,
does she come to lead her holy dance
which will make my Olympos again,
and you, deserted land, a world?"

And the farseeing Mesa, the Mesa stirred
inquires and considers, and opens
its myriad mouths and speaks
and its speaking like wild
birds passing, crying, from heights:

" Or have not the people—Slavs, and Huns,
and Tauroskyths from the Danube
the distant Volga, the woody cliffs of Borystene,
the depths of the Baltic, the silence of steppes,
have not these people been densely stirred

and descended, like leopards and locusts,
that their returning might leave no vestige
to east or west, of race or fatherland?
Or are the tonsured wolves again
descending on me, noisy from some ascetic
hunger,
some mystic rage: descending on this world
here,
so fairly made, which lives with
a holy living still,
marked still by its persecutors
but forever straight and young,
calm and untaken; on this world here
with a single blow
downtearing us ruined?"

And the farseeing Mesa, the haunted the Cliff
watches again, is shaken again, and with all
its myriad mouths speaks forth, and its tongue
like a blasting of trumpet, the charge of a horn:

" I behold; the tread of an army; I behold the
brilliance
of weapons. Crosses and eagles, shields and
spears,
and labara,
and from all the clouding up

no bursting epiphany,
Homeric god.
The cloud is dust, the feet of horses, of infantry
have woven, and all goes upward,
thins, grows thicker
inweaves the men, and shines them
in hollows of the sun.
And thousands of roads the sweat
has carved on these bodies
and in their glances burn fires of a thousand
wars,
a people unmeasurable, sudden,
that shows it does not advance
to record new blood or destruction,
but comes in joy and pomp to a certain
religious adulation, a festival mighty,
and at this coming the earth capsizes,
totters. And I behold . . .
Its leader a giant straightbacked rider
apart in the midst of all,
and worth, that one, worth all.
Tell me, surrounding worlds and heavens,
who is the giant, who from where? Royal his
clothing.
And others beside him like him are kingly
dressed,
but none wears the kingliness he wears.
Around is a kingly throng, but one is king.

Noble his visage, noble the form of his soul,
and brilliant the joy in his eyes, their looking
even, pure, and striking—for in them
reserved no hidings of wile, no braggard con-
  fusion,
and his laughing's breadth shakes all
of his heavy frame, and on his
ethereal forehead
Thought is the leader, Pride the judge;
his gleaming visage, his columned neck
that rises in mightiness over his shoulders.
It is a tower
girt with a garden, his hair on his head its grass,
his beard a rampart of gilded silver
and at every shaking of spirit that angers his
  thought
he raises his hand to his beard with force
to seize it in handfuls
as though in his struggle he seeks
one holding point.
His chest a foursquare shield, his body—
I see myself—not made for infantry tramps.
Such body, for the rhythm and thrust of a
  stallion.
And on that stallion, incomparable, rider.
And on that saddle, rooted and lovely as I,
ancient, as carved from creation
which pours an unbounded fullness forth

on its measured works.
Straight on the slopes, straight in ascents,
forever the same with his steed in rising,
  descending,
in walking, in running, in charging—the two
  at one,
as though they made struggle to fly
as one.
No Alaric he, nor Dexippos,
nor the Apostate's dreamed of fallingstar,
nor Skythian torrent.
But full with knowing, granite throughout,
his race of the finest, and it shows
like distant kind of our own,
and nothing there is to make you call
him the shade of the last philosophers
with their will-less will
bent low over tombs.
Inform me, heavens and worlds here
circumscribed, inform me,
you rooted—palely, firmly—you asphodels,
outside this life, in the thought of dream,
and you, you olives through the day who flash
leaves' eastern silver, the sapphires of day;
and you, naked plateaux, aerial rises, you
  stones,
Ionic springtimes, Doric metopes,
inform me, heavens and worlds, who is he?

And, heavens and worlds,
if you cannot answer
let me call him Olympic, and shout:
" Ares you are, yes are!
You are Ares; and though you
arrive from foreign, from wild outlands,
and act the outlander, no outlander you.
The sweat carves thousands of roads on your
  frame,
the fires of a thousand battles
burn in your glances,
though perhaps you have changed, have come
with another name,
assuming another language,
you lover of war.
I guessed you, you came, you Ares.
Are Ares and come and enclose in your heart
with original power the same great Greece
and yet more deeply you hold in your heart
the arrow of Eros which burns
which drives you to Aphrodite.
You longed for the goddess. They said:
' She dwells on the Mesa.'
You came.—"

EIGHTH WORD

But Aphrodite is marble, Kore a phantom. Cliff
an icy mystic fear has leashed your speaking
and the gods and heroes you fear
they too are marble phantoms.
Some wandering
word was spoken, handed from ancient time,
that in some sunset the born in Xanthos,
Apollo's holy, the comer from Alexandria,
reached the land of Kore, and drinking from
that source
which gave to Socrates, that's still
today called Fount of Socrates, rose up
to you, who adulate Promachos,
to you the Virgin's mystic,
he Proklos the Lykian, last prophet of the Greeks,
so formful, recalling the god of day,
who had come to earth, a shepherd in hire of a
king.
But he found your castle closed
and around it guards.
All was dried out, a desolation,
soulless, soundless.
And only the nested storks up there
in the rundown temples, among their nests,
asleep, astonished, ask: " Your name,

stranger, your country? Your destination?"
"Strange birds you are;
from Xanthos the holy, from Alexandria,
Chaldaian I come, and Orphic,
and struggle to Pallas,
unshaken in worship, with the eyes of my soul,
this triple I—of Athens, Athena,
and of the world,
philosopher, poet, and hierophant."

"Stranger, your Pallas is driven out by another
maiden, lonely, unweaponed, from far,
joyless, untouched, as though submerged
in a ruddy veil
and a tunic of blue
without a spear or shield, or dreadful gorgon,
with a child in her arms, her hand on her heart,
grain-pale, and sweet and tremulous, a humble
one, a widow; as if tired, impoverished,
alone, and tearful;
not tall, nor short, yet seeming
existent entirely on slope,
a slope that is growing that spreads, that
slowly unfolds
to miracle.
At her hand's mere outstretching all
lie prostrate before her

and bend, knelt down, beneath her hand.
Her eyes have only to glance; in her glance
immortals, men, and marble
were melted, were weathered away."

In silence the prophet flees, retreats in thought.
His hut is built at the foot of the Cliff.
And from his window opens
creation, Athens, white temples and there, beyond,
the field, in shadow, olived;
beyond, the sea;
and over the darkness of the field the moon
over Saronic water, over the houses,
over the marble, moonlight pours;
its brilliance poured, like dream, and saddened
poured a final time
on the tremendous land.

Proklos, at home. All night awake.
Wakelessness choked him, the fall
came whipping, thinking consumed him.
The middle of night. A knock.
All ears!—Who knocks?—
He listens. The trembling of voice.
" Make ready the house. Receive her.
The Lady is coming.
Will stay with you now."

" I have no way to go, no shelter from night.
Let me sleep here, and leave, at dawn,
swiftly in flight with swallows and cranes.
Driven from my creation. Stranger
and outcast on my own throne
in my own possessions.
Madness the way *she* came,
inclined, and humble,
that evil magicianness, ach!
How she changed, how grew! Assuming
my face, my name, my air
and all my amazing spirit.
With weapons she beat me not.
But her visage destroys,
and that daimon
she holds in her arms!
Her eyes a cursing! Who shall describe them?
Olympian smiter, defeater of Titans,
Achillean soul, a nurse of the Word,
See Me, See Me green pale with fear.
To foreignness now, to exile.
Among the Kimmerians, Laestrygonians.
I seek my refuge,
will live as breaker of bread with Skyths,
with the Kynocephalic will weave my loves;
they will be less split of mind,

more faithful, than men.
An owl they will find me again
and loudly at night I will mourn
in the trembling of night over ruins."
Then, peaceful man, more holy (somehow)
than the goddess herself,
in your depths you found words,
and addressed her:
" Lady, my house will be ready,
forever, for you. And more,
incomparable, whole, a further dwelling,
my being.
Your tomb today, tomorrow your fort;
my soul.
I shall close you in,
you will live with me deathless,
and my soul too immortal
a tiniest breath of your breath.
And your hour will come again
you will come from within me
as a queen emerges from suddenly
opened doubledoors of her palace
revealing herself in pomp with all her courtiers,
a startling to every eye.
And the world, bereft of you, will gain
you once again more potent
more renewed with youth.
You are taken by exile, but not by death;

the Lady of what has been
and what will be
you are."
So he in his home, his temple,
ascending as temple over all temples,
at every moment before her,
vigilant, adulant, kneeling; himself
and beside him—as though a woman—
one like a hamadryad
Asklepios' daughter beside him,
thought's final prophetess,
his perfect pride, this woman,
jewel of virginity, lily of wisdom.

With astonishing dawn she goes,
a mist.
And never returned.
None saw her again.
But you the Lady of Present,
perhaps of forever,
Lady of Golden Daphnes,
great is your grace!

Anatolia: numberless cells are guarding
despisers of flesh, deniers of world,
those humble monks, those holy hermits

in Syria, Palestine, Kappadokia,
above on the Holy Mountain, that fortress
untaken,
from there to the Thebaid, that firstborn home of *askesis*.
And in midst of all, set down
on the flanks of a slope, as though
it too grew hugely with the cedars
and facing the sea, in the shade of a forest,
the holy and famous cloister Kecharitomene
containing its anchorite, a rare creation,
the praise of the Hesychasts, the cloister's pride
who has settled his life in this spot,
and lives it, completely the song of a prayer,
the deathing from silence,
a great art's fountain
and that art painting.
The cloister upon a slope. At its feet creation
which the trees bear forth, the fruits increase
the rivers water, the nightingales lull;
and servingly it yearns as though it longed,
with all its laughing greenness,
its greenness in winter, in summer,
to kiss the feet of the sober cloister.
Foursquare, weighty,
closing, the cyclopic walls; at its center a court,
and the cells, on every side, four storied,
and the towers above the cells,

and in the courtyard's center the highdomed
church,
church raised now many years
by its graced founder, who was king
came to close his tear-worn eyes
eyes glutted with light, and power,
with living, battles, and folly.
On those carved columns, those swirlwreathed
heights,
in the struts and breadths of the walls,
in sanctuary, Holy Altar, ciborium,
wherever the mouth of the faithful, as though
for kissing, trembles,
as though touched by the coal
of the biblic prophet
by the fire that burns
and cleans, and where the mouth
of the faithful kisses,
and no eye pierces
the church so full a forest of numberless ikons, relentless, rigid narrators,
from the Pantokrator to the holy martyrs,
the visions of Israel, the drama of Christ,
and more, more dense, more felt,
the Virgin's wonder.
On twoleaved, threeleaved ikons,
on ikonostasis
on glass transparent, on works in wood,

on the softness of silk, enamel brilliance,
with wax mosaic, and iron—with all
the skill of pencil, the craft of the burnisher,
with all the colors the place permits, that holy
place,
from the rose's scarlet to the gray of smoke
on miniature coffers of ivory, tombs
containing their saints' remains,
on sumptuous Evangelaries, shining with gold,
on gold, on silver, on leather, goldleaves,
the life of Maria lives, the Virgin's glory.
She lives since that hour—naive but
chosen since that time—when she returned,
dewcovered, with her crock
in the land where all is peace and languor
and Tabor you behold like a woman's breast—
from then to the hour when she
unrivaled was raised
above the seventh heaven and stood
before the holy Triad, as though almost to rival
those;
she honored, adored, a thousand hymned,
a queen midst Cherubim, a lightsource of
what-is.

And the walls, what they reveal!
What the ikons say!:

Behold! She sits before her loom, and weaves
the purple,
and it is the temple's purple, and she the
temple's virgin,
and there—behold!—six like-aged girls beside
her,
attend her jealously, watch her amazedly.
And angel Gabriel brings the lily clipped
in a mystic spring, that angel,
that greeter that Overseer.
And see! She prepares to drink, raises the cup,
that water the test of her virginhood;
if she has fallen, that water turns flame and
poison.
Be silent, mouths of the faithless, of the claimers
that kiss has soiled her, that man has known her.
Her soul is pained, her visage hurt,
and there in the spring of her eye a diamond tear.
A fullbeard ruthless priest awaits.
Delight for her enemies, her friends distraught.

Au fond

God's temple showing slightly. Midcenter, a well,
and in it that dreadful testing water;
on high an angel with despot's scepter
extending enormous wings to cover.—
Now look! Beside a cave. A Syrian cloak

inwinding her unfull body, she raising her hand
to her bitter, tear-ready face,
and over the ever-virgin
head a six-rayed star,
that trembles as though it struggles
to become her crown.—
And look!
On a royal throne the Virgin sits,
on one side of the throne, on the other,
angels faithful and slave surround, and serve her,
angels two; above, the Breath of the Lord,
a brilliance riding the clouds, descends.—
Behold! an endless heaven. And signs of the
 heaven,
a moon of silver, a golden sun,
and over that heaven, god on her knees,
with sun for face and moon for breast
again and ever the Virgin on her fame's throne!
And over, above, behind, around
her prophets, evangels, apostles, martyrs,
ascete kings and princes, of holiness,
bewhipped by their discipline, from ecstasy
 matterless,
bodies bent-down, minds rod-straight, and
 higher—
the blessed, the just, in gardens of heaven,
resplendently leafed with their trees,
enclosed by topaz walls.

Some hold parchments, some read books,
and the parchments tell, the books proclaim:
" Protection of man thou art, and glory of angel,
and in your joy, Graced Being, creation
rejoices! "
Surrounding the mighty fresco: from all
sides watch, fly up, hymn loudly, gleam, and
vigil
the Potents, the Thrones, the Powers, archangels
and angels;
their lightning a saber, flesh their ray.

At Church the Monk, apart though among
the other *fratres*, a cypress feeling
apart among the bentbranch willows,
higher, lither, darker, with a certain
mystic motion, incomparable grace; that one.
At Church. His hours are silver beseechings
on golden ikons. Church. And his mind
like the trace of an incense by Mary's visage.
Church. Now he labors, like the light that burns,
the sleepless light. Labor those too in cells,
while others are plowing fields, or weaving
reeds,
bronzeworkers others, or weavers of belts of hair.
While our man labors on paper, and puts to
paper—

adorning the Scholar's Word—which tells
of the Virgin's marvels—in the monkish book
adorning with drapery of color
with the charm of beauty
creating it groom, that Word—
writes down childlike stories
these fictions supple, of grace unnumbered.
And over them, golden heaven brightcolored,
rose and plum and ash and whiteness of snow—
with all the ornament and fineness
that air and ocean and mainland give to the
painter.
And on the pure fine paper he recounts
the Holy Maiden's life and final sleep
that painter calm and patient, peaceful and
docile,
silent, sad as before a coffin,
from the walls of the temple, from all its parts,
with prophetic glance, he knowing by pen,
updrawing his sketches, and in his soul,
with the breath of love, transforming them:
they appeared at the head of the holy book
like firstseen leaves, like firstborn leaves.
To the cloister he'd followed the breath of what
fate,
he gloomy and bent, extinguished, worn,
but showing within his gait and bearing
something distinguished, noble, some youth?

The growth from a noble root. Florins,
  feudalities.
Rich man.
But richer yet with the fear of God.
But his mind like a darkened cell, within
it something dark, slow to move, unready
to learn;
forever his knowledge at odds with his will,
to him Christian dogma, the pagan wisdom,
were puzzles unsolvable, swallows, which
ever he reached his hands to seize,
and yet all fled.
But in his soul he grew heavy and strangely
his thinking's darkness ruled him like guilt
till he grew loathing of life, denied the world,
in cloister put on the angelic way,
gave all his possessions up, threw wealth away:
" You light me, prayer; receive me. And you,
  my penitence,
You make me holy! "
His teachers, in vain, the monks those catechetes,
a useless teaching, lessons lost.
Unlettered, untaught, he remained.
Psalters, evangels,
camps with excluding portals, he always outside.
His will subordinate, his mind rebellious.
And a single learning, one treasure of wisdom,
his poor mind held and muttering it

each hour, his lips set trembling, each instant,
(and whenever the sacristan struck the semantron,
at wild midnight, and summoned the brothers)
and when he awoke to semantron, or slept at
sun's
own sleeping, at dusk, in vigil, at dawn,
in refectory, temple, cell, at table,
one lesson alone, it caught by a phrase of words:
the angel's welcome to Her, the Full of Grace!
And only when he had nailed his eyes
to the ikon-frame, and around, to the walls
and columns,
and moved his eyes and opened the deeds,
those thousands of praised and painted deeds,
then each like a waking of heart he knew
and each like a winging of flight.
And see! as artist he,
gradually, slowly with time, and slowly with
struggle,
but more, and startling, rapid, artist
by Lord's own pity, and with his praise.
And like some bird of the North, some foreign
untamed bird,
that cannot walk, turns first to flight,
impeded by his feet in walking, tripped,
his wings that block the route, greatwings,
that know the heights of the air, to pour their
thrust,

like them that monk; his mind a winged and
foreign bird.
His school? The church!
His letters? Ikons. See!
Paintings his knowledge, the Virgin his thought.
And nothing more. Aphasia, ignorance. And
always
a mist that fogged his thought, that sealed his
mouth,
and upon his lips there trembled, only, faded,
and stirred from night to day
that twoword song in all
the echoings of the psalm: Hail, Graceblessed
One!
He radiant then from joy and pride
of the word—no pleasure for him, no boast
that creative brush he held and governed.
Nights, and days of festival, days of labor, he
spoke
through those plain holy words: Hail, Blessed
One!
Then came a time when the painter of Mary
could no more govern his pen on paper;
one power was left: to fall knelt down
at the Lady's image, wherever he saw
it, faintly murmuring: Hail Graceblessed One!
On earth all else was senseless and false
till his fearful unfled hour came; with those

same fragrant words and on their wings he went,
saved from the body, a blissful soul.
His remnants sweetened the earth that took him,
over his tomb the fragrance blossomed, and came,
that waft, to the cloister in double flood, and was
on every side like a spring, was wealthy,
incredible. And one time in a lively
prodigal April, a fastidious May, at novena time,
the miraculous came. A lily, white,
grew up over his fragrant tomb.
And on those lily leaves, goldwritten words
were brilliant, read: Hail, Graceblessed One!
Incredible, that lily's fragrance;
the Abbot runs, cries out: " Dig downward,
fratres,
open—O Miracle!—the tomb. Oh Lord, your
Might!
From where can it come, where flow,
joy's golden spring that springs
from the Lady Forever Virgin? " They dug
and opened.
From the corpse's mouth it grew,
that lily's bloom.
And in that mouth a whisper
gently, song: Hail, Graceblessed One!
They took the body lightly, felt,
and found the lily's root in the heart of the saint.
And buried inside his heart, a painting

astounding, the Virgin's image.
Hail, Graceblessed One!

Mother of all who despair, protector of all,
before you the hopeless, all, are one!
So through you the world has become; its
wealth,
its treasures of power and joy, of wisdom and art,
all these he denied for you, becoming for you
a world impoverished of thought, and naked of
knowing,
simple, uncultured; and fled,
a monk, to your feet, before you ascetic,
his life an attrition, his mind a cloister.
Before your image that world bends down, with
mouth
in tremble, suspensed from your name alone,
from your protection, Maria, and from your
glance,
with mystic air, a quiet murmur,
infinite phrases: Hail, Graceblessed One!
The first world you submerged, the world of
wealth,
and from it grew the goldspeech lily,
and carved on its deathless, candid leaves
the praising words: Hail, Graceblessed One!
And now the world is shown

as the mouth of a buried saint,
the vase of a mystic lily, and on the heart
of the world—from unknown ascete to Bulgar-
  killer,
the victor who climbs to pay his praise—
and on the heart of the world
are You, the Mother of God,
are painted in brilliance.

NINTH WORD

And ever the Doric temple, simple, immense.

Yes simple, immense. But within
the simplicity, greatness, stigmatized
by his blind eye, harsh hand:
the Nazarene. Just look!
Snowed dove, it came, it struck you—
that hunter's arrow.
As though in beauty's sky you had
no setting, you who are star of art.
You set and took
on sickness as though from a foreign seed
and the treasure of what was pure
now a bastard growth;
one dome of your holy
polytheistic brow
a crown for laughs!
So a king barbaric, the mighty Constantine
became Apollo's butcher, destroyed that lovely
god,
and on the beheaded body of marble, that
whole—before it
he placed the form of his royal head . . .
and see! monstrosity now,

that statue once grace of the world.
Yes, simple, immense. But within
the greatness, simplicity, stigmatized forever and by whatever
passing will change;
by what, advancing its foot will trample
the Seed, the Race.
Each time a pitiless Fate
will smash at the Race
that Heart of the Race, the temple,
will take the blow most deeply,
first,
be shaken at root,
be crushed.
Like a widow queen,
a slave, she will follow,
dragged by the feet,
some foreign lord,
be given to him,
exchange her faith.
Byzance will make
the temple Christian
the Frank will catholicize;
Moslem, she'll wear the turban;
each race poured
across her for plunder.
Behold! Sea struck in her holy body's height!
The Venetian's fire.

She'll burn. A ruin, will fall.
Then—who will believe?—
a final master, the Scholar,
will descend on the ruin
that holy ruin,
and defile it.
A bat his thoughts,
a sickness his mind.
My God! In vain through the furtive night
  will come,
bewailing, in silence,
the ruined grace of the temple,
will come the idolatrous moon.
Till the Poet will come
a gleaming muse at his side
observer and mage of the ruin
to build
with the help of a ghost, his song,
to build in the scholar's despite
a crown of the Word again, in east and west,
the Word's own temple, the new foundation.

The Temple changed faith. There where Time
  draws
back its hand, and passes lightly, respecting,
see impious man approach and touch
lay hands.

How reckless your hand that touched, Byzantine
artist,
the Athenian maker's faultless rhythms.
Closed that portal which poured its river
of sun—from the east—on the wonders within.
Now windows are closed—to transoms,
they too closed with their thickwidth shutters,
fearing—they seem to say—day's entering light,
a foreign
body, pale, transcendent, mystic,
lest it reach within.
The catechumen chambers here; the women's
quarters above, with cypress-cedar roof.
The naked Dorian beauty is freighted
with striking garments. Byzantine
adornments on Attic columns.
The high vaulted apse a roof
for the Holy Altar. The pronaos sacred step,
and baptistry that altar stone ornate
with fruits and wreaths, with steerheads, flowers,
vineleaves. Forgotten, across from the ambo,
an an-
cient throne; for arms, twin sphinxes.
At the golden angels these marble sphinxes
enigmatic, gaze; and one wing-
bearing lady, in the hidden smilax leafage,
above the throne's carved back, reveals
her pagan face, her startled eye.

Above the altar, inset in a niche, profound,
portrayed mosaic, apart, She shines.
Upright, and unadorned, and no
crown needed.
Nor child in arms. Alone. And formed like art,
a final Olympian memory, by Attic craftsmen.
A tunic hiding her body, perishable body,
hangs deep to the feet, hangs green,
and her plumbright robe
adroitly doublefolded, spreads, and falls,
below the knee to the left, fanning like wing.
And simply bent to the right, bent back
on that right foot, she lightly turns
her other foot, and holds with her hand—her
left—
that rosy veil, to her faultless breast.
She stands as meditant, as though
awaiting cherubic chariots
to flee, to journey.

But look! Her hymn is raised
by heavenly chorus, a holy song.
From soul of man to column of marble,
all is a worship's offering,
and trembles like leaves or wings,

by the unquenched golden taper
of the Lady of Athens.
Teachers and priests,
empty rhetors, empty sages, artmen parrots
of ancient language, who make haunted lie of
  life,
and hatchet beauty and scorn the true
to the Emperor bend, there take their stance;
Byzantine vapid sounds they weave to his praise.
And you, you Emperor? He listens but does not
  hear,
sees nothing, although
pretending to see.
Under cover of mortal power,
in expectance of grace,
he flies with prayer's wings;
and that prayer is strange, bears on its wings
a warjoy flame, a mystic dew.
Twovisaged; monk and pilgrim he prays,
his habit's blackness covered by
his golden armor.
And two inequal choirs attune that prayer.
The first, an enormous life.
And in it turn, shine brilliant, weave,
resound the sounds of the world.
The second strews dreams ecstatic . . .
The incense musk is white, from golden
  encensoir.

Around, the loud procession has broken to birth.
Here there is simple psalming, but there rough
shouting.
The king is silent; a prayer. A soul.

" Hail Mary Lady of Athens, calmer, fairest
of the fairest, the calmest throne among thrones,
the conquerer, you, of Athena, and Athens'
protectress!

My breath is war, and my thought itself.
Above and below lies war, the Kosmos fills
with ruin, devastation. Creation, Lamia;
wherever
I cast my glance, or turn my remembrance, all
I perceive, consider, is war.
I come upon Charon.
Slowly a rain of blood came down, and storms
and hail
were poured, and roared, and the counties were
widows whipped and bent over newdug graves.
And rivers and seas and lakes were frozen
by ice—an ice than which only death is harder.
Then from east and west an earthquake, up-
rooting,
destroyers of towers and camps.

And the mighty cupola goes,
the crown of Hagia Sophia. An astonishing wave
of the Strait grows violent, gnaws at the mainland,
and the gate that girdles the city, double, triple,
from the Seven Towers to Vlachernes' palace,
keeps, in its stony body, the earthquake traces.
And palaces totter, ready to tumble, god-
blessed palaces, and below them moats, yawning
to swallow the splendid palatial ruins;
and from one thricehigh house was saved
one standing wall, and it too ready to tumble
had not one planetree reached its branches,
a column, a holding strength.
And in my soul I said,
a hard man softened: Some pale green lives
untouched by ruin, thus, when great
things slip and fall, assist those great
things, holding them from the earth,
however ungreat those pale ones be.
Such strength, support, my life has not found.
Famine, drought, and hunger are raging.
The City seems taken by flood,
the comets are flailing their manes
as though they were threatening a Vile Creation,
and meteors fall, foretelling a doom,
and the sea foams over, and pours to that column,
the unreached camp
of the ancient ascetic.

Apart from the things of the world,
straight column himself,
a column of thought and distance
and like his thinking's depth
death in a plunged abyss he found.
The wave.
And the world was stricken and cried:
' How cruel your anger, O Master! '

And over them all, and more than all, I stand;
and from me
war, forever war with friend and stranger,
war with the Arab, war with the Russian,
with the Bulgarian dog, with Franks, Iberians,
Northerners, Westerners,
men from the East; war
with brothers, with servants, confidants, foes,
with sages, logothetes, and with rulers, I first
to take arms against falsemind men, against
thieves,
and with my kingdom's twin and godsent
plagues, Bardas Phokas and the other Bardas;
war with a hundred thousand, war with all.
And that implacable war, the heaviest struggle,
the war of me with me!

You, leader of every war, interceder in peace,
Oh Lady General of All, to You winner's spoil!
Heavy and slow to quiet anger eats me,
and sometimes its slave and sometimes its lord
am I.
Of sweet and noble bearings I have no knowledge.
What I have been and what become! The
miracle yours,
All Holy Queen of Athens, in your fortress
clothed
on every side, with outpoured light, such light
as never welled through The City, that mother
of brilliance.
Whatever I was, I was born to rule, and the
others—
the great, the small—to obey me, for Fate has
written,
my hand has written; like a Fate my hand.
Oh God! Digressions and faults of youth,
more thoughtless and dooming each time you
advance
to snatch the life of the regal born
reducing it down to the life of the others
to roll it together with common passions.
Me wanderer over the land the winds
have known, the frozen dew, hard sun, the
storms,
me rake, all night carouser, wild,

under heaven's stars, in royal suites,
on paths, in caves, in passes, clefts.
Comfort and softness know me;
in clashings of sword, *tournois*,
I hunter of deer; I thiever of maids.
I open handed, a spender, an uncontrolled,
know all;
insatiate embraces and all night vigils.
And suddenly: Look: my very life cries out:
' Stop there! ' That same life turns me back,
with violence.
My hand that knows,
gives its force entire, turns back the carriage,
just when the startled horse goes
hauling, raging to the abyss; and horse and
driver and chariot
are returned to the road's broad stretch, to win.
And behold the Hard, behold Phokas, and see
beside me the men of intrigue,
the murky, the graceless, guerillas,
commanders and generals of night's high armies.
Cursed though you be, may you be praised.
Me the drowsy pilot, you waked, gave sight,
and steered my ship and drove it forward
beyond seaswamps and beyond the shallows,
past indecisions, delays, evasions, corruptions,
to opened seas, to facefull of tempests!

Lady with you woke joy and perished curse,
God took, with you, the Infant's beauty,
the old world changed, the new was built.

Incredible dream arising in undermind:

Around me I saw, and knew them all,
the same by their stance, the same by their gait,
the same in their ways and dress,
in the distanced echoing light of the passed;
and saw in the cloud of the unborn ages
Caesars and servants, nobility, kings,
as many as came before me, or follow after,
seated on princely steles, on purple thrones.
Their hands, their feet, their bodies; the hands,
the bodies, the feet—of men; their heads
the heads of beasts.
They lived. Made litany and psalmed—
a demonpriest before them—psalmed Satan's
praise.
Advancing slowly they groaned, and howled,
and wailed,
wild beasts, and asses, hyenas, urangutans,
and wolves; bears, prodigies, and kentaurs.
And each face showed its soul
in the form that was right for it.

Shelter of being, more vast than the world, in
  darkness
a guiding and fiery column, a harbor of soul,
a river that flows to us honey and milk.

How to remember all, to recall them all!
I novice, untried, not knowing the world
first turned my thought to a namesake,
first watched my Commander-in-Chief.
Within him a soul as huge as his frame!
No other could bend, like him, my scale.
My leader, tutor. I told him: ' Go on, good sir,
go govern and rule for me, as though I were
not, and you were born on this throne! '
I only neglected to say: ' Go forward! I'll watch
you calmly, attentive. Will observe you
not as your judge, to pronounce you winner,
  to crown
you with wreaths of the circus victors;
will observe you, to follow you later on roads
you have broken and opened, instructive to me,
to come where you have not been and to go
  beyond you.'
That teacher assailed my ears
with words of some God knows ancient—
  forgotten?—

wisdom: 'A life is like combat; in combat
only the many compete, the chosen observe.
And they are above the many; a single chosen
worth a thousand others.' Now you just hear,
becoming yourself my pupil, attend,
my teacher, attend! I've grown, don't think
me rash:
among the many, some chosen; but over the
many,
among the chosen, the potent, higher,
higher than chosen, the powerful, higher;
the straightstance potent, the first to examine
in meditations, original thinkings, depths, and
peace,
each a chariot driver, each a contestant,
forever awaiting, forever awaiting,
adroit and swiftly in time, that they, those same,
might pour down ready for combat, instructed
for all,
for closerange wrestles and distant roads.

Ministre d'état I made you; you never said:
Enough!
But daring and thoughtless and wild
though you were
how found you mind, how figured indeed
that thing which is truly not,

would be fault by its mere existence,
that something which could not be done
would be monstrous when done,
that I should be second, and you rule me?
Though you raised yourself like a cedar, it's I
who am woodman with axe that batters, hews
cedar down.
And with a single nod, without delay I saw
your greatness and you, a heap, before me.
Pity grew foreign, and goodness my foe.
Something went dead. Sometimes now I
remember
how brilliant a funeral I readied,
for a being loved,
and proceeded and dug and buried
your heart,
which was mine.

Hail holy and living book that the Spirit
has sealed; unwithering Rose, a throne of Fire!

Purely and strongly to simple, to grand ideas
I offer a solid flesh, turn all things to real,
which were smoke and dreams; while around
me on every side the pure and the mighty and
those

who proudly—like me—maneuvered both scepter
and sword,
the royal, the generals-in-chief, who pass
astounding
go wandering at random
in hunting of clouds, in battle with shadows.
Ah mystic stalk, you grew an
unwithering flower;
the sun of all knowing has chosen
you chariot.

My darling is poverty, though I am the lord
of wealth,
and little suffices, for me to have much.
You brightest ally of destruction, gold!
Lamia corroding all mystery, haunter, whose
wings I have clipped and hidden,
whom I hold as my thought's own servant,
my slave.
Full are my palaces, my treasuries all
in sunless crypts and hidden cells
outflowing with silver, purpura, gold,
with whatever the lands of Iberia gave me,
with whatever—it endless—I took from the
Syrian Kaliphs,
or stole from the Kelts or received from the
Skyths,

with whatever I gathered from others or found
  of my own
in open battles or secret assailings.
What harvest astounding, beneficent harvest
for times that are ill, which finally press down!
Deeply I dug, hid riches in wells and in clefts—
as the corpses are buried in Egyptian tombs—
and I piled and scattered my pearls
and my emeralds and diamonds
in places for hiding.
And nothing from these was for me, for adorning
  myself,
for presenting, and my hand
I never outstretched for the touching; their guard,
strange guard, indifferent insatiable, I,
who observe and am miserly ready to spend
  them all.
I scorn and adore them both like something
worthless yet worth the world;
for in one instant this nothing may grow
like something ruled by the breath of the lord,
may become
a creation of weapons, of ships, of youths, of forts.

Wherever you fall you heal idolatry's flame;
Dew, for you my hymn, my singing;
in saecula saeculorum.

Far from me all that makes nothing
but slaves, but tightforged bonds,
that witlessly strives to block
the speed of the stronger; far from me these!
Freed from the empty advice of a friend
still more from the dirty passions of woman.
And I became blackrobed monk, of deed,
whom all draws forward with cross and sword.
And as I stripped you free, my soul, from
softness, from boasting, from all, and sent
you with all the sheen of your nakedness forth
your nakedness hard, and rough, and male,
I cast from around me, put off from my body
the jeweled, elaborate, and shiningly dyed
fair clothes, the cloaks, and woven fabrics,
for all were unfitting, unworthy of my new
life,
my jewelless, ascetic, and newfreed life, which
goes,
which goes devoted to highest idea, ascends
all lightly, and tolerates nothing to weight
its ascent. Now mind and soul, and flesh,
and visage, a oneness in many voices,
which endures unchanged; the one psalmer I;
my wand (my own) has inwound voices,
and instruments that serve my vision.

Maiden, you show lovers of wisdom foolish,
and fool-
wise the rhapsodes of lovely myth; you Maiden
Who wove wreath unwoven by mortal hands.

Take some fragment of my power and go
and gather the pieces the casts away,
you unlike brother, who drink then sleep it
heavily off,
embraced in your smaller passions, closed in
by song.
My heir, this one? Lady, do grant it not,
that he should inherit my sword!
It would fall from his hand, and be taken
again
by what—god knows by what—strange torrent?
And if the Lord
should command his angels to
gather it up—this sword—who knows
in what land it will find itself, will meet
in what distant lands what
other's hands,
what warlike hands that will snatch
one day my sword, to smite (with it)
my own guts in my own land!

Better forever that it should be lost
in the depths of abyss!
And now, while I live so live yourself, my unlike
  brother,
gathering buds on meadow roads,
and spend in the marble baths, in
the golden courts,
your incensed feminine life
with sycophants, *hommes de plaisir*;
and play through the lovely hunts with your
  falconers,
and fodder the hounds to catch your stags,
and live—that the gorgon
may suck your blood (and your life)
away.
Drag your steps wherever the open road;
waken dust of the constantly trodden road.
My own road I break myself, am the first to
  stride,
am ever for other places and reach them far
more far a limit, a border, and know it in joy,
for Digenes am I in fact, am Akritas.
I travel East, I travel West,
and wherever the passes, I guard, where gates,
  I besiege,
and forever at distance—with naked sword—I
  hold
the foes of the Hellene, the faithless, the other.

I am the sudden northwind who thunder
across the trees like the trumpet of godly
presence
and scatter the darkened clouds and drive
them far,
and broaden the azure heavens.

Higher than heavens, foundation of earth You
are! "

TENTH WORD

" Bardas the Hard he was, the manliest peak,
who was worthy for deepest thought, and first
in deed,
whose strength was kingly, whose arm was steel,
arranger, destroyer, creator of wars.
Bardas the Hard he was, a klepht, a border
guard,
great insubordinate, the wrath of God, a sickness
that sets with the dawn and rises at evening,
the frightening, the crafty man with words of
honey,
the skillful mannered, who knew how to bind
the heart of the simple fighter to his sword's point;
the idol of faithful and faithless, of every
tribe come out from Sahara or Araby.
And a time there came, when he cut
my road by the mainland, my road by sea;
with all his weapons,
his weapons yet stronger than mine, he bound
me tight,
me the watcher me lord
of innumerable lands, in serpentine folds.
But when his hour was up he appeared before
me, himself unpowered and blind, a specter,
a fragment,

and fell at my feet, and begged for my pity.
As maleficent spirits, subdued, restrained
in the grasp of a potent man, abandon their
weapons,
their frightful weapons, and loosen their willing
tongues
and instruct their conquerors with useful words
thus that man opened his mouth, and gave me—
gave to protect me—intelligent counsels.
Coming from his own mouth they did not surprise;
thoughts I'd sensed in his heart already, already.
Each summit upraised to my height,
—he advised—I should batter down
and if I should long for weapons forever
brilliant and worthy
of my own hands, my orders,
I should hold forever these hands
from wealth's temptation,
its ruler and master forever I,
no instant a slave to coin.
Pure my palaces should be, and free
from the stain of woman; a demon's noose,
the greatest
is woman; unnearable cliff of ruin may I remain;
and whatever I hold in thought, I should not
display it to all.
(Like medicinal plants that kill,
yet in hands of the wise are sources of healing.)

Yet I have a wisdom from life; time granted
me knowledge; and mind over heart formed
speech,
and my knowing, and wisdom, and ' word,'
O Virgin,
have been blessed by you. And in the school of
the world
one power—a teaching power—occurred in me,
and taught me the letters unlearned by others.
Lawgiver, minister, general am I,
council and strength are from me, my command
the law.
Woman is ever my foe, woman is lie,
the abyss is woman, though not from her being
more wily, more black, than her husband—the
mate;
unmatable, unlike is woman
in the evils of being
since liar she is, so angel; since abyss, so infant,
and she breathes, God's Mother, as though
it were your breath breathing through hers.
No son of woman am I, nor offspring of man,
(take pity, My Lady, extinguish my blasphemy's
flame)
no man, but Kentaur, must he have been
who birthed the clan which brought me to the
world.

My foe is the unwise wisdom of the falsely wise,
all slayers of life and stiflers of truth.
Foul growths, grammarians, rhetors, and lovers
of wisdom,
with swollen words and empty skulls,
you weavers of airy and mindless hymns.
Death is lovely from what
within it has strange, immortal, and unexplained, and you—instead of
harvesting lilies
which bloom more greenly among the tombs
(for hearts, with tears and blood, have watered
them there)
instead of studying the world that passes
reflecting by shadows of cypress undying
the world forever the same, forever changing—
you bend
to the tombs, you shake the bones, you finger
the worms; from the corpse of that death is
your life.
Ground down into ugliness, you
and taking for ray of the truth
the skeleton's pallid light
the lightning worm
you—ever blind—to whom remain unsaid, unheard
all the good and beauty, revealed or hidden,
of God's creation.
The tongue that thunders within my word is
the tongue

of the laborer, the simple men, the young leventes;
this tongue—no kin to yours whose words are
colorless always, like corpses, embalmed.
My rosered language stirs
like the play of a glance, like expression it changes,
for in the speech of the simple, when given
its strength to flower, the Holy Spirit is breathing,
leads reasoning and hands to giant deeds.
Your rhymes and epistles and all your writings,
an evil growth—you windbags, pedants, and
   amateurs—
a nothing, compared to the scorned,
the unwritten evening song which chants
the shepherd descending from greenside
   mountains
the song sea takes and carries and ends
in the slowly extinguished day that greets
and listens.

Lady, confide me not to the doubters,
that doublemind men
be not my defenders;
and hear my prayer.

Bardas Phokas, the star of leventes,
he shone from the light of the other Phokas,
   the King.

And opposing the other Bardas, beyond him he
reached
in the strength of his hand, and the height of
his frame.
And ever he stood up tall on his legs, and kept
his unresting vigil, a steed with balls, forever
like something that sniffed and studied through
distance.
A genius at piracy, craftsman at ambush,
unmatchable taker of forts, and dragon of wars.
Poor man whom *he* took with a wounding blow.
With the blow he took the soul was cloven,
with his voice, his earthquake voice,
he shook the army.
Temptation flamed in him, to ruin him then,
temptation and cursed phantasy, and coalblack
pride,
and in his rage he trod, like nothings,
his victories and wars and chivalries
in Antioch, in the camps of rough Kappadokia,
the Armenian borders, and on to Bagdad,
and he put on the purple, wore the tiara,
and wore the scarlet imperial slippers
and allowed them to raise
him—he scorning his oaths—on his brazen
shield,
he denier of kings, his country's destroyer.
And he came—that rebel—to the Sea of
Marmara

and neared me daring, with pride; my country
saw him
before the fortified camp of Abydos;
as longing to run the oceans
he flew to the place
where I tented, awaited him there.
And I saw what a twisted man is like,
what a graceless man,
where the faithless is hidden I saw,
where the traitor hidden,
and my generals I saw around me, all, and they
mere forgeries, liars—by day my obedient
servants,
at night keen diggers of pits, for me to fall.
And my very own I came to hate, and the Greek
I saw at my feet like a worm, a onecelled worm,
and to that stranger I turned: ' My own you
are,' I said,
' come running to me, Varangian: Tauroskyth,
help me;
adieu, delights, adieu to the body; my faith
is gone,'
(though scarcely the first manfuzz had
bloomed on my face), yes
Saraken; it's better with you, with you a lover
of idols,
you loyal in war and loyal in helping.
I go to be battered by war, and roasted in sun;

and in one hand I grasp the sword of that war,
in the other, embrace your reverent ikon,
Mother, you worker of wonders of arms, of All!
There by the fortified camp of Abydos.
En face.

With his Iberians, a chosen thousand,
considered the infantry finest, the world's,
all tall, and shining, of equal heights,
as though the Creator had measured them equal,
fellows with knifethin growths of moustache,
with cutlass in hand, with arms, and bodies
and feet
all spirit, and drive, and tameless; with these
he surged
before them, apart like a valiant a captain,
surged straight at the king, me king, with one
hand raised
swordbearing hand, against me; no time he lost,
but showed he had come with the axe to batter,
and was like a cloud brought on by winds
a storm of winds, and in that passing
the plain was shaken.
With sword in hand I awaited
and my weapon grew soulless and weak, but
another
weapon upon me took soul, took power; the

weapon I stilly embraced with my other hand,
your ikon, Lady, your gracing, Mother!
I saw Bardas Phokas; the encounter was not
between mortal eyes, but amazement and vision
it was.
I watched as that rider fell from his horse,
like struck by a sudden arrow, a hatchet of
lightning,
and there unwounded, untaken, downtoppling,
drawn
down to the earth, dust's toy, and on
him crowd pouring down, and striking, and
ripping,
at now headless object fallen in mud
and I whom
they brought his battered head
for offering.
An unseen hand assailed my foe, but it I saw—
that archangelic hand, that hand onguided
by you, You Lady of heavens.
And forth you broke, from
on high, and revealed yourself, transcendent
general,
a darkening and dreadful protectress, as in joy
you are shining, however blissed, each time you
appear
in Power, All Holy, holding onbreast The Holy
Infant.

And on my own breast, I saw your image
taking the motion of life, becoming my soul.
And from then I remain, forever in thought,
as though that hour struck me too forever
as encounter with nereid's glory
strikes the nocturnal passer
and snatches his language.
And I from that time have the eye of bird
whose seeing cuts darkness, who sees through
night.
As though I see things unseen, and speak with
shadows,
and from them grow mystic and laughless
as though collected within, and wound on myself,
as though I suspected
suspicious in every direction.
My suspicion is endless; my anger is evil.

Among the crowd some chosen, among the
folk my
favorites I draw, demarked with a fitting honor,
those particular leaders of Art, those spirits of
Word.
Masters of art, musicians, painters; come now!
Come now, creators!
Painter, advance with singing; musicians,
take aid from the painters, advance;

go forward! Give hands, draw
breath as companions, and hymn, recount
the rooting of Lady of Athens here,
the growths she has spread in the world from here,
her life, assumption, and miracles—all.
Now drowned in musk, become—rayshedding
  Church—
like an allwhite cloud, from your mist let come
(in place of archangel ranks, that the prophets
  have seen,
ecstatic to see them appear in the shining clouds)
let come forth holy measures, ikons symmetric
  and sacred,
such. Raise hymns, you singers, and you—
you makers of ikons—behold the church, adorn
from top to bottom its flanks,
with Virgins of smiles, Virgins of weeping,
with laughless Virgins, with gusty Virgins.
And under their feet, for their treading upon,
draw me, the ruler of war and of conquest,
in the allgold heaven a scarlet sunfall,
with my thousands of foes, my hundreds of
forts; a treader of foes and of forts, destroyer.
And when they are ruined, those foes, those
  camps,
below the feet of the Lady dispose the greenness
of paradise, the wings of angels, the stars of the
  sky.

And wherever in my huge passing, Triaditsa
to here, to Athens, I paused for a while
in a hollow, on a height, on open space, in shade
for resting, leaving the tracks of my horse
still deeper imprinted in earth—O artknowing
makers
make sacred my tracks, take gold, and raise
at my own command, to the joy of the Virgin,
adorative shrines, and churches, and cells, and
chapels
that time may rejoice, make mighty my passing!

I brought vows, offerings; treasure;
emblems which your own grace will
make finer yet
will make priceless jewels of your dwelling.
Behold white and allsilk cloths
from Palestine
the booty of Achrid, Prilepi, and Prespa;
the vases outpouring with golden
denarii;
rugs of Damaskos, the purple weft;
and lamps, and chandeliers, and communion cups;
those all,
and garments of rulers, and habits, and veils; one
after another, weighed down with gold
and with silver,

filigree, carvings, adornments of hand
(fine hand)
email,
with animals, beasts, and flowers, and monsters;
and over them all
the dove of gold and the lamp of gold
the dove all flight, the lamp all gleam,
the dove a soul, the lamp a breath.

And from all the names you took from all
those places, your wonders, your particular graces,
names raying like your brow's glory,
balsam like your own countenance
deep like the springs of pity and mercy
which are your two eyes,
I take—they numberless—and return them to
  you,
scapulars, offerings, smoking them richly over
glazing them nobly with images worth my soul
holiness, my faith. All Queen, Who Pities.
Lover in Sweetness, Ubiquitous, Healer, Freer
There, Seer, Fulfiller, Leader,
Who Answers,
              Noonsun,
                            Swift in Response,
Romaic, Athenian, Seen,
Tower goldwoven, throne suntarred.

Rainbow your belt. More vast, more sumptuous
you flooded the sky; path you, more great.
Wearing sun for garment, moon
for footstool, around
your hair a twelvestar wreath.
At your side strike wings,
strike eaglewings, to pour
from the light of heaven to the night of hell."

" I beg you, my sorrow is heavy, I cannot resist
the arrows of Satan, no roof protects me,
they assail me from every side, oh Refuge of Men!
I know not my own defense or where to flee!
The victor is hopeless. The Polity's Savior
now inconsolable. You: Hope consolative.
From my own and other men and from demons
from all that have hell for a country
I am dangered, am cursed.
Realm and Race and Church, my People, the
  Polity,
Holy Mother of Mercy, all hang from you: have
  pity
and save us, you Savior, you Peace you Calmness
of all who are whipped by storms
who are persecuted.
Ash may the impious be who scorn to revere
you, holy depicted, in wonderful ikons;
apostles have drawn them with pencils of angels.
Higher than heavens, more pure than the sun
more rare than the Cherubim, more praised
than the Seraphim, you vessel of holy Mana.
Our sins have grown full, from our failings our
bodies have sickened, our souls have grown sick.
Now open some gateway of pity, oh Mother
  of God!

Why is my sorrow so deep?
Because, for an instant, you took me
unlikely recall from the back of a dream:
at the palace window
appeared my image, leaning.
The giant palace of Bosporos, Thrakian,
a world chaotic, but ruling, surrounded by
ramparts.
The City, an ecstatic abbess bent
at the palace feet,
and beyond her for servers the outskirts,
and her the crosses and domes created and
lightninged,
the domes more thick than trees, and hiding
the verdure of vegetal growing.
Passing, from plains,
wideopen plains of Thrake, passing you
moistened me,
air. *Au fond*, broadopen, allgold Kosmidi
appeared.
And see! beside me was found straightstanced,
an announcing angel, an *ange* of the unexplained
more vast than the world I noticed before me.
He touched me, I trembled. He breathed on
my eyes,
I saw. And one of his wings was a volume of
bronze,

and in it shone—a miracle—laws of Fate.
The other wing was a magic mirror
on it spoke blackly times that were not yet born.
It had a visage that played and shifted,
shown triple, like the sea that sometimes
encounters
and gleams then shows its green then brings
in black. Sometimes it looked like the angel of
God,
sometimes archangel of the abyss; sometimes
the Commander-in-Chief who bears my name.
Triple the specter with one, then with triple,
visage,
with murmur, itself a triple, as of water brought,
of water sweet, salt water, from the center of wells,
the near, the distant, from wells of thought, of
dream
from raging, triple. The murmuring thus:
' At the Goldengate wideopened, that gleams,
await times heroic, heroic from your elegant
passings
of trophies and rulers, await—
they would sing your praise and crown you
with crown that no man till this day has worn,
the enormous Triumphos awaits, and Glory
angelic awaits you, Lady Steedmistress.'
Your City: like almonds it flowered from shore
to shore

it dressed like a bride.
Your City, that City of all the world,
that you should go passing above her,
treading her, Lord.
Her palaces stand in the sun and array
their sunless bridegifts to greet you;
homes and huts are palaces now, and all
are proud, are virid or white, are making your
fete.
The allsilk robes, the velvet rugs,
the embroidered cloths, all strewn on your route;
wherever your road is unstrewn, they strip and
strew
you the earth with their cloaks, those rulers
and workers,
and for greeting or adulation of you
all flags are waving, are air; the laurels *coupés*.
From the walls of the camps, and over the towers
the watchers of ocean, surveyors of fields,
wherever
they settle their eyes, wherever they question
around in the four directions, of birds, of clouds,
of tracks, and wherever they turn their eyes
and wherever their thought goes wandering,
all things give a single reply; all are
a single announcement:
' My City, high ave! Thou Lady of East and
of West! '

From mainland to coasts, on all of the highways
a gaggle
of roads—unknown and roads known, and the
traveled
as well as the just-cut-through, advance to
The City,
stride straight to The City
with the good things of Europe, the richness of
Asia,
and the roads are yours, obey,
are filled with your name; the infantry, chariots,
horse
all are your own, all faithful to you.
Nowhere are enemy arrows whistling
and wherever the foe is found, he goes
ayoke to your wagon;
of many races your army, the tribes of yellow
and all who come down from the Baltic, the
steppes,
and sunburnt Africans, Anatolians, group-
ing of every tribe and faith, in hire to you;
Slav, a slave, and Latins who aid, and Alemans;
halfdistinct darkness, the Turk, is still in the
distance.
The Greek is captain; Byzance his support.
Bewarned, you Goldengates, bewarned you
Triumph! From night
to night, like spirits of evil, vampires,

like infected breaths from the rotting of tombs,
outpourings from graveyards, growings of evil,
apart are waiting,
are waiting, a crowd, to be poured through night;
are waiting till you
step from your horse, on foot advancing
to the journey, huge journey, of no return.
The mob awaits for your eyes to close
that all might be ruined again, that the world
might be left to the soft, to the halt, the cowards,
the world you increased, that you nursed with
  blood,
that you gained with the sword, by victory
  achieved.
And famished thievers will fall on your vineyard,
eunuchs, and pimps, and nuts,
clowners and whores.
In vain Vlacherniotissa, raising her hands
to the heavens, beseeching the heavens, in vain!
She has aged, Vlacherniotissa, hands
now only for useless beseechings,
not as once, combating, for shooting
the foes, the brutal foes, of The City. Nor
for capsizing unfaithful armadas.
The cataracts will be opened, be loosed.
The clouds will burst. Volcanoes will spit
their lava. With their wings, the winds
will sweep all in their passing, northwinds, scirocco.

With you, over you, rages and earthquakes and
plagues,
infirmities,
curses and ruins; you place accursed!
From Africa waves, from Skythia rivers
have swollen, have flooded, have broken the
dams,
and your roads, my ruler, the traveled
and the roads first opened by you, which carried
the goods of creation straight to the lady our land,
now destroyed those roads, now taken away,
and on all sides hurricane, deluge on every side.
Streams and marshlands, swampground now,
where once advancing you trod—and your
treading
the mouths of the world returned in echo,
those trumpets of praise—so deep were
your passings, their traces imprinted, you said:
' They will be there forever! '
That lady released to the teeth of her fate,
she boast of a thousand years, the crown of all
nations,
and within the water's rage, like a roofless
isolate house, unguarded and unassisted, which
flows
apart so that none, from forward, behind,
from any side, makes an old board plank
for bridge, to run, to reach

to become some trace of
an aid, salvation,
a something.
In Venetian ships, in African galleys
from Frankish forts, from Levantine shores,
the Latins, the Normans, the Kelts, the Mongols,
the Turks!
Just look! With the papal cross, the sultan's star,
each one is the other's leader, his runner-ahead.
Those brothers!
And The City, that city of the world, surrounded.
Taken. It goes,
it goes. See the Lord's own temple. Stable
bedunged
by the enemy's horses. A whore now placed
on the throne of Chrysostomos, a strident
announcer
of the devil in the flesh. The chasubles horse-
coats now, the ponds now troughs. See! Destroyers
of all
are all. Maligners and killers of all that has worth,
that is holy. And the Holy Altar of Santa Sophia,
rare altar all fair, is seized; more loot
in the galley for France. But the wrath of the Lord!
A total—across from
the Isles of Marmara—a total destruction.
The galley goes down.
The altar goes down. And around it the ocean

gleams like a sun, is without a wave; its
waters are myrrhed and calm celestial.
And the exiled polemarchs, the fleeing armatoloi
like indigents cursed, and naked, nomad, without
 a country,
consuming the bread of exile, and to pay
for that bread,
instructing the foreigner, handing over the swords
secrets of victory;
then dying, these exiles, graceless;
the foreigner glad to be
left with their wealth. Culture, weapons—
O wretched Romaiosyne!—
from Anatolia driven, now settled in Europe.
Rebloomed on the Alpine slopes, once Attic
 violets.
From hugeframe gathered legions
of thousand tribes, of thousand tongues, of a
 thousand flags
under that one labarum ready: In this Sign
 Win, O monarch
Eater of Bulgars, monarch unsmitten;
of all this nothing will stay
of what you create, make one, control, and define.
Belief in the Christ, retreat! Races stand up
and be numbered!
Saxons, Russians, Norwegians, Gauls, Italians,
 Spaniards!

Foreigners hired, the king's flagbearers, go each
one now for the raising of his own flag,
go slowly, slowly, with the flag
of victorious
fatherland.
A tribe this group, a people this tribe, then
behold the Nations!
Latins and Slavs and Germans,
with their weapons, their knowledge,
with boundaries growing, with giant dreams!
And the rare, all lovely, holy Altar
of God, is pulled from the depths of the sea,
a fishing portent, of the worthy fishers of France,
and every miraculous part of it scattered
to west, and south, and north. To all the people,
to Man!
And over the German, over the Latin,
over the Moslem, over the Slav,
over all of the blond ones, the upraised Nations,
with boundaries extended, with enormous forts
which stones no longer construct, no towers
crown, at whose feet no moats are laved,
nor are lighted, as before, by
murderesses' eyes . . .
camps and towers and crenelations and moats
are now Pyrenees, Apennines, Caucasus, Urals,
the Rhine and the Danubes, the Thames and
the Seine,

Black Seas, the Atlantics, the Baltics, the Whites,
the immenseness of oceans, the seas that take
on the longing of various dreamsoothed lakes.
Behold those seas, their mountains, the rivers,
 the thoughts!
New world. Great change in the art of weapons.
You infantry, horsemen, alas all you onetime
 heroes.
Rust now, you swords of Damaskos, javelins
 wear away,
now useless adornments of walls, you bows,
be gone, good luck you bowmen; so long,
 leventes.
And you, poured Byzantine fire, amphibious
 serpent,
to Satan's aid, enclose yourself in a bullet of
 black,
and assail without missing, mark out, and strike,
and harvest without an error, and from afar,
the worthy unworthy, yes all—the armed,
disarmed, the cowards the heroes.
And over the blond blond nations, the raised,
 upraised,
with boundaries broad and carefully measured,
on the royal tomb of Hellas treading,
and making it pedestal, appearing—above
it—ever yet higher, the balance of Justice
of Wisdom the source, the power, the grace,

the lady who rules, the mistress, yes over these all
with her name alone, her fame alone,
still more with her form, her light the first of
them all,
the empress who hears and is hymned
by the world's high changing: Europa, Europa,
Europa!

'Tell me, you depths of the ocean, what pouring
forth?
Aphrodite again, a second time?'—'That
goddess?
No. We are bringing Atlantis to light again,
that island imagined in dream, that island itself
a world.'
Athens exists no longer; Europa exists. Give her,
Europa, from out of your inwards to her; who
is newly
appeared. Your old and familial world is narrow.
Virgin oakgroves, traceless fields, and cataracts,
and seas,
more mighty than you, below you, and with you,
behold the children of Atlas, the children of
Atlas,
they come, are sowed, exist,
grow up, make harvest, procreant in freedom,
the new world's lords, the old world's dread.

But immobile the Yellow, for centuries, ages,
in the shadows of unspoiled lands and untouched
peoples
like a serpent glutted on human flesh
forever seismic in motion, forever mortal in
striking.
And crafty he turned, instructed, the White
magician's best pupil,
and knowing of magic, unshakably struck
and turned into snake with wings and became
a demon
and longs to return to his work of destruction,
again,
that as Genghis Khan, that quake, he may shatter,
like Tamburlaine scatter destruction.

More miraculous yet than the world of Atlantis,
and
greater than Asia the Sibyl or Europe the Muse
a founder of lands that are tropic and polar and
hyperborean, revealer, kratarch of them all,
a body of money, with diamonds for eyes,
with a heart of marble, demonic and faultless,
see him, King Mammon! The portent, antichrist,
serpent and eagle together, assuming all faces,
like that prophet whose flock were the seals of
the ocean,

who lived in the depths of the ocean. You snatch
him and wholly he flees, turns to foam and
nightmare;
yet there where you scorn him, you worship him
ever.
But that time came, when the giant paid for
his crime
despite his power
which all the earth could no longer contain.
Poor ones dreadfully wounded, poor ones
pitiable,
like a crust in the sand, a reed in the plain!
A light shone out, and you knew yourself. Enough,
strike forth, you serpentess workers, strike, you
workers avengent!
Just see! Just see! the raising, the largest raising
that is
has been, the raising up of the poor! Tight-
chainbound
you were slaved by the serpent, made servant
and slave
in hollows and caves, a gypsy a beast of burden, in
fiery furnaces, sunless caverns,
in crowded workshops, elaborate factories;
those workshops were palaces, the factories
subground cells,
and all were the chambers of hell, were cells
and palaces.

And Mammon, a closing! A death! A chattering!
Aid!
To his call, you standers to east and west,
innumerable, armed, with his commanders
his polemarchs before you, each of you, Nations.
And see! the warlike muttering, see! The
Miracle huge!
Whiteclothed angel doubling his wings
above the swamped, the sacked,
that country of drought and of solitude.
' Arise! '—and a bolt of light, transformed,
arose from his wretched tomb
the humble, the ragged, the scorned,
the unknown, surprising, laughless, the stranger,
hater, pathbreaker, ugly, mere man, mere man!
Of labor the king, the father of poorness,
the lord of the world. Guardian of all is coming,
is called the Lion of poverty, is a lion indeed.
He comes, the inheritor comes, wields sword
and an urn.
The jar being heavily filled—with the tears of
the poor.
The Lion of poverty comes, wields sword and
an urn,
and the table is set and the candles are lit,
the inheritor comes in the fullness of time,
wields an urn, and wields sword, to slaughter
the Nations!

You serpent, Mammon, beware! Peace be to
the world
and brotherliness to people, and joy and thoughts
that are wise, on earth! Thrice lovely is labor;
and the world one City.
The rewarding dispensers, commanders of
penalties
go, fateful gods, the gods who are rulers,
the gods are no longer creators, nor idols of
fear,
nor actors on stage, be it tragic or comic,
under thousands of ugly and beautiful masks.
They go.
Creations of man's own mind, though that mind
of man, that poet, cannot reach higher,
the gods (those creators) themselves became
makings of man,
transferred to unreachable heavens of form,
those pearls of our dreaming, those diamonds
of what
we can never explain
—yet standards of deed, yet swords of our
suffering.
Single gods and many gods, the critics,
and tyrants, specters, and
Valhallas, Olympos, heavens, the Edens, all go,
the Saviors and Queens. Now, Soul, you know
that after the ages of ages, the time after times,

a Charon has come, unexpected, Destruction
destroying the gods.
They've sunk, been lost, and no harm done
to the Giant Kosmos, no loss of a stride,
no leaf from its green, no hair from its head.
And within the outspreading of endless chaos,
  of the
measured creation, all things are released,
rejoice, commence their dancing, turn in fair
  rhythms,
and the Sun is the first of the dancers.
Is crowned in gold
plays fiddle, guitar, is chariot-carried? No.
Behold it, the Sun, a star of hugeness; and the
  only gods
who are living, who are not in their graves—
Athena, whose name is now Wisdom, behold Her!
And Aphrodite, whose name is now Love, who
  is poured
up in foam from abyss, all naked in foam:
that double goddess: the whore, the divine.
And you, disarmed; Athena? Athena, no;
  but Wisdom,
a book you are clutching, and bending above it
you read and with pen of iron on pages
of steel you are writing;
a globe that your foot treads under, treads
and apparently spurns

and the globe is a star, and the star a world,
and it turns;
your eyes, your terrible eyes, still eyes of an owl,
are lightning, are heavens, deep deep, are nights.
Fixed, unshaken I watched the face
of the messenger specter, the triple, as though
I were not
myself, and the eagleeyed mind of another were
in me, and drove me to speak, and I found such
words,
and I said:
More open the heavens, more giant within
those infinite heavens outfold
the settings of sun; the more the breezes
the interstellar,
the more our mists are like sudden terrors;
from inwards the mists of mother ocean
are raised, are filled, and, clouds, bring
on a worldfull of darkness, and cutting winds,
and storm,
disaster or flowering, creative, destructive,
all to fall down once more to the inwards
of ocean the mother, from water once more
into water,
now pure for all their disturbance;
these clouds, these signs—
in the globe's own flux of revolvings—
of the law of the ruler of mortals and men, of all.

In the ocean of time are poured the rivers
of progress, and are lost, but the ocean holds
firm
and with all of its movement, and drinks down
all, down all. Behold it: the source and the vortex.
Forward, and backward, are nothing. A choir
with the spiraling wind's own feet.
I said: In the whole, a returning of all. The
rulers,
people, slaves, the masters, and gods, and men
cut all—
through obstacle, weft, or war—all roads,
that some may be ever kneeling, and others
that upright forever they be. In this creation
the world
on every side, and petty man in the world
man halfway laughter of being and halfway its
pride;
the law they obey: and on hearts and on stones
is the law;
here one face it has, there another,
but is everywhere ruler who rules, and jailer
who chains.
Autumns and springs, and winters and summers:
the gnostic hours go bearing them, take them
divide them in order and bring them again,

the winters and springs, forever known hours,
(and the tyches, carelessly, blindly, sometimes
in vain)
the autumns, the springs, the winters and
summers,
the depths in the soul and the breadths in
creation.
And always a hand that drives us; that drives
the inertial flesh. Forever the great man there,
and his history
by him with gait like his own; you do not
understand, where those two advance,
tight sailing together, do not understand
which is leading the other, is source of the other.
But whether ruler or governor, captain or hero,
the captain—incomparable—and the ruler are
ever the same.
Such a one—who knows?—I may be; I am,
I was, and will be;
now declare that I'm duped, announce me for
mad.
Few the faithful; few the wise men of dream,
meditation; yes few among many, few chosen turn
upright and disputing, bent and in study.
Ineffective the roadguiding Muses, the magical
Sirens.
Neither rhetor's thunder, nor breath of the lyre
can change the course of the Polis.

The Polity—War and Force draw it on
to flowering up or sickness, to waning or waxing.
And nothing can hold this back, in appointed time,
in the coursings of races and souls
can hold back
this ebbing and surging of tides.

But I am War the destroyer, the great,
am War; and I do the will of a maker
greater than I, in whose hire I am.
Trees and foliage I tread, uproot, and all,
with fire, a founder in blood;
I shape and burden
the winnowing floors, that groan
with their fruits of the summer
and harvest. But I am War, am War.
The Nations will live forever, forever will labor,
the struggle ever to greatness, to power.
Behind the prey the hunters, and ivy choking
  the trees.
Conquerors forever, the conquered forever.
Irreconciled first, the hostile, and reconciled
  later
in the unending dance, against the foe who
  will come
himself with his horde, in the fullness of time
to consume the possessed and possessor.

And the raisings and ruinings, the wealthy, the
poor,
are thrown on the scale; forever the scales going
up,
going down. Praise to God in the Highest,
on earth be there peace,
and in man good will! Of a Highest is ever the
worship,
but mortals are ever the serpent's evil
and peace but a bubble on water. The Gods,
the summits of all, ever and everywhere
Virgins and Christs, and angels and demons.
These are ever the unseen's meteors, ever
in paleness, unwritten, of thought, the figures.
Forever the gods, the earth and the skies ever
full with these.
And I shall exist forever; when I leave this place
I shall be elsewhere, unfleeable, returner, will
be
one sealed with whatever marks, with whatever
name,
a guard of the camp, a faithful to
Hellenism, there I shall stand, a sword;
a will, I shall there ordain.
The will and the sword of the Greeks. And that
will
will be armored forever with blade, and that
sword with mind.

And a holy breath I will breathe, released
from my opaque flesh.

I said! Wherever Romaic is breathed, is spoken
by Greeks,
wherever the tribe is lightning, and drive
can be found in the nation, in nations of nations,
wherever, into ages of ages,
in dispersal, in falling, in cutting, in night,
Romaic—wherever you hold, and Hellas,
wherever you fail,
whether Polis in some huge land, where world
is of lands and of oceans, of people and places,
or in hut of a slave, in a cell-low land,
in the midst of tables of gold, in the wolf's
isolation,
on Byzantine thrones or in Attic ruins,
in the purple of kings, in a stolen cloak,
wherever are opposition and cross and wake-
fulness,
sword and the road, I shall be,
a soul, and a breath, I shall breathe, I shall live.
Mere carcass, I'll sing with my epic song,
a foreign flute's upspringing from my own mouth,
a fluting for laughter which, transforming,
will make of the stranger's laughter
liturgic hymn.

A king of marble, and I shall awake; from the
mystic
and unfound tomb which will close me, I
shall emerge, unlocking the founded Gate of
Gold,
and will run, who conquered the kaliphs
and hunted the tzars,
and far, near the Apple of Gold I will draw my
breath.

The triple specter went down, mere vapor.
But sin, a stone.
I beg of you Virgin, my suffering is deep,
you harbor of sinners, you joy of the world,
give pity, my Lady, extinguish the flaming
of infamous language in me.
Temptation has itched me, has raised me to
heights,
has shown me from heights the realms of this
world,
and with all of their faults and their hugeness,
and I have not sealed my ears, have not closed
my eyes,
have become in myself an antiword
to the word of temptation.
My Lord, I have sinned!
May your will be done!"

TWELFTH WORD

Silence. Concluded the song. Around it creation
in ruins, in the clefts, the pass, on the plain,
as though a broad and resonant harmony
startled it, vision, and tongues, and a whipping
of eyes,
of ears, creation that falls asleep on the breast
of silence, creation an infant
easily terrified in mother's arms.
And silence comes stirring again, palpable
almost now, as after a furious rain
which has fallen for hours hard, and echoes
with all
of its echoes, and pounds with the thrump of
a bull
in the rivers, and moans through the branches,
a bat,
like a maiden, cries through the silence
outside the windows: then
swells and swells; suddenly passing as though
it had not existed.
But look, and hear! A sound from the road,
down there,
the Galata road. The news has reached to the
king.
Arrives.

He comes, and with fitting honor; bearing
to Basil the Killer of Bulgars
Persian embroideries, rugs from Bagdad,
Venetian gold, and silk from Thebes,
Anatolian flowers, and Syrian myrrh,
sumptuous winding-sheets, and royal head
cloths fit for his second funeral,
more splendid than the first.
Golden sand has garnished his road, they strewed
it with foliage; asperged it with attar of roses,
incensed it with perfumes, the eunuchs
enshrouded in white
pass slowly, astonishing remnant's
appointed attendants.
In the white of the sun your wand, praepositus,
glistens.
Upraise the hymn, you singers; approach,
you bearers
of myrrh! The rows of nobles are chanting blackly
mourningly dressed. The coffin of gold.
The manglavites are holding the dibitisi
the carven crown, the scarlet slippers, that naked
the glorious king, despite his cadaver's
corruption,
that naked he not lean back in the tomb.
The procession nears. Beyond, wideopened,
the wealthy,
capacious and royal tent is awaiting.

And the standard of Paleologos the victor who
goes
to recapture—The City? The City? God no!—
a phantom, now frozen form of The City that
was,
the standard of Paleologos the victor is waiting
to greet with humility, bending down low,
that king who was sunk and lost, like us all,
in the ocean of night, and suddenly, wonderfully
comes to the summit of ocean again, and stands
like a specter,
skeleton's shadow, roofing
them all, they more constricted than he.
And look! Just look,
the procession walks into the chapel's ruin.
The tomb wide open,
stockstraight those bones at its wall.
In the skeleton's mouth the flute.
Your hands, my king, you reach toward the
bones.
In vain. The instant your hands make contact
the remains fall heaped on the ground,
fall ground themselves. And onto them
dumbed, the flute of the Muses, a reed
for throwing away.

Glossary

Akrites: border guards of the Byzantine Empire

Antartes: volunteers in an irregular military force, usually devoted to rapid political change

Armatolos: armed guerilla fighter

Charon: here, simply Death

Dibitisi: short imperial cloak

Digenes Akritas: legendary, and most famous, border guard of the Byzantine Empire

Hagion Oros: The Holy Mountain, Mount Athos, the center of Byzantine monastic piety

Klepht: Independent, unsubdued Hellene; in classical Greek a thief, later—as during Turkish occupation—a resistance fighter in the mountains

Labarum: standard borne by the Christian emperors of the Eastern Roman Empire

Leventes: as noun, a handsome, manly young fellow; more frequent as adjective

Logothete: lawgiver at imperial Byzantine Court

Manglavites: Byzantine courtiers

Pallikar: boisterous, manly fellow in late twenties or early thirties

Pantokrator: The Ruler Over All; Christ as customarily portrayed in the apse of Byzantine Churches

Peplos: simple woven cloak, often—as on the Parthenon frieze—used for ceremonial occasions

Polemarch: a general

Porphyrogenitos: born of the purple; title of the sons of the Byzantine Emperor

Romaiosyne: Hellenism, as it was called under the Turkish occupation

Romany: name of the Byzantine Empire after 476 A.D.

Semantron: wooden instrument, used in Byzantine churches and monasteries to summon the religious

Skete: monastic-ascetic dwelling, often a cave or hut

Tyche: agent of luck

Vlacherniotissa: epithet of the Virgin, as worshiped in her church at Vlachernai, just outside The City